FRANCIS FRITH'S
TOWN & CITY
MEMORIES

NORTHAMPTON

MARTIN ANDREW is an architectural and landscape historian and writer on outdoor matters; he is the Conservation Officer for Wycombe District Council in Buckinghamshire. He specialises in the landscape of lowland England, and combines his love of history, landscape and architecture in his writing. He has walked and toured Northamptonshire extensively and has had several walks in the county published. He has known Northampton for many years and seen it in its sad years in the 1960s and 1970s and now in its thriving revival. Since 1978 he has lived in Haddenham in Buckinghamshire with his wife and children; he is a keen long-distance walker and enjoys riding his classic motor-cycle round the country lanes of the Chilterns. He has written several Frith local history titles.

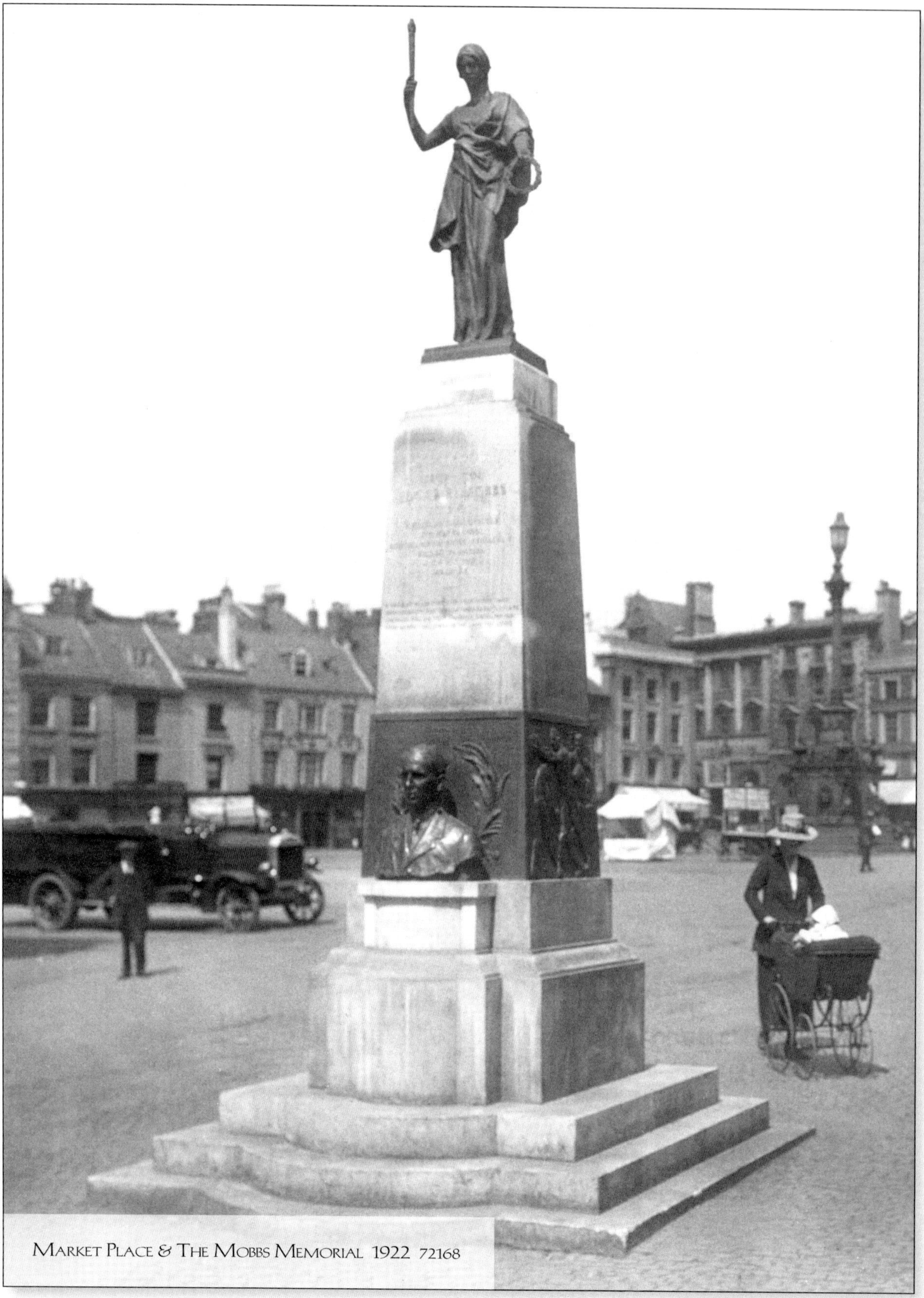

Market Place & The Mobbs Memorial 1922 72168

FRANCIS FRITH'S
TOWN & CITY
MEMORIES

NORTHAMPTON

MARTIN ANDREW

FRANCIS FRITH'S
TOWN & CITY
MEMORIES

First published as Northampton, A Photographic History of your Town
in 2002 by Black Horse Books, an imprint of The Francis Frith Collection
Revised edition published in the United Kingdom in 2005 by
The Francis Frith Collection as Northampton, Town and City Memories
Limited Hardback Edition ISBN 1-84589-072-8
Paperback Edition ISBN 1-84589-037-X

British Library Cataloguing in Publication Data

Northampton
Town and City Memories
Martin Andrew

The Francis Frith Collection®
Frith's Barn, Teffont,
Salisbury, Wiltshire SP3 5QP
Tel: +44 (0) 1722 716 376
Email: info@francisfrith.co.uk
www.francisfrith.co.uk

Aerial photographs reproduced under licence from Simmons Aerofilms Limited
Historical Ordnance Survey maps reproduced under licence from Homecheck.co.uk

Printed and bound in England

Front Cover: **NORTHAMPTON, ABINGTON STREET 1922** 72171t
The colour-tinting in this image is for illustrative purposes only,
and is not intended to be historically accurate

AS WITH ANY HISTORICAL DATABASE, THE FRANCIS FRITH ARCHIVE IS CONSTANTLY BEING CORRECTED AND IMPROVED, AND THE PUBLISHERS WOULD WELCOME INFORMATION ON OMISSIONS OR INACCURACIES

FRANCIS FRITH'S

TOWN & CITY

MEMORIES

CONTENTS

The Making of an Archive

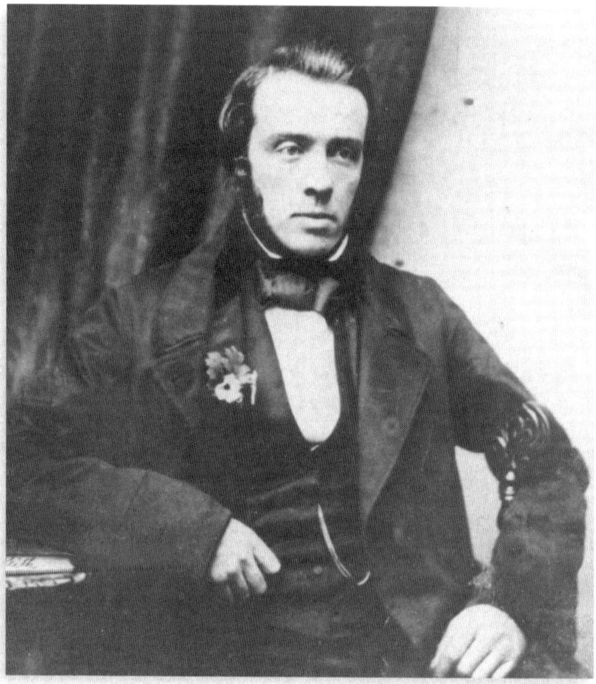

Francis Frith, Victorian founder of the world-famous photographic archive, was a devout Quaker and a highly successful Victorian businessman. By 1860 he was already a multi-millionaire, having established and sold a wholesale grocery business in Liverpool. He had also made a series of pioneering photographic journeys to the Nile region. The images he returned with were the talk of London. An eminent modern historian has likened their impact on the population of the time to that on our own generation of the first photographs taken on the surface of the moon.

Frith had a passion for landscape, and was as equally inspired by the countryside of Britain as he was by the desert regions of the Nile. He resolved to set out on a new career and to use his skills with a camera. He established a business in Reigate as a specialist publisher of topographical photographs.

Frith lived in an era of immense and sometimes violent change. For the poor in the early part of Victoria's reign work was a drudge and the hours long, and ordinary people had precious little free time. Most had not travelled far beyond the boundaries of their own town or village. Mass tourism was in its infancy during the 1860s, but during the next decade the railway network and the establishment of Bank Holidays and half-Saturdays gradually made it possible for the working man and his family to enjoy holidays and to see a little more of the world. With characteristic business acumen, Francis Frith foresaw that these new tourists would enjoy having souvenirs to commemorate their days out. He began selling photo-souvenirs of seaside resorts and beauty spots, which the Victorian public pasted into treasured family albums.

Frith's aim was to photograph every town and village in Britain. For the next thirty years he travelled the country by train and by pony and trap, producing fine photographs of seaside resorts and beauty spots that were keenly bought by millions of Victorians.

The Rise of Frith & Co

Each photograph was taken with tourism in mind, the small team of Frith photographers concentrating on busy shopping streets, beaches, seafronts, picturesque lanes and villages. They also photographed buildings: the Victorian and Edwardian eras were times of huge building activity, and town halls, libraries, post offices, schools and technical colleges were springing up all over the country. They were invariably celebrated by a proud Victorian public, and photo souvenirs – visual records – published by F Frith & Co were sold in their hundreds of thousands. In addition, many new commercial buildings such as hotels, inns and pubs were photographed, often because their owners specifically commissioned Frith postcards or prints of them for re-sale or for publicity purposes.

In order to gain some understanding of the scale of Frith's business one only has to look at the catalogue issued by Frith & Co in 1886: it runs to some 670 pages. By 1890 Frith had created the greatest specialist photographic publishing company in the world, with over 2,000 stockists!

The Making of an Archive

The picture below shows the Frith & Co display board on the wall of the stockist at Ingleton in the Yorkshire Dales (left of window). Beautifully constructed with a mahogany frame and gilt inserts, it displayed a dozen scenes. The ever-popular holiday postcard we know today took many years to appear, and F Frith & Co was in the vanguard of its development. Postcards became a hugely popular means of communication and sold in their millions. Frith's company took full advantage of this boom and soon became the major publisher of photographic view postcards.

Francis Frith died in 1898 at his villa in Cannes, his great project still growing. His sons Eustace and Cyril continued their father's monumental task, expanding the number of views offered to the public and recording more and more places in Britain, as the coasts and countryside were opened up to mass travel. The archive Frith created continued in business for another seventy years. By 1970 it contained over a third of a million pictures of 7,000 cities, towns and villages. The massive photographic record Frith has left to us stands as a living monument to a special and very remarkable man.

This book shows Northampton as it was photographed by this world-famous archive at various periods in its development over the past 150 years. Every photograph was taken for a specific commercial purpose, which explains why the selection may not show every aspect of the town landscape. However, the photographs, compiled from one of the world's most celebrated archives, provide an important and absorbing record of your town.

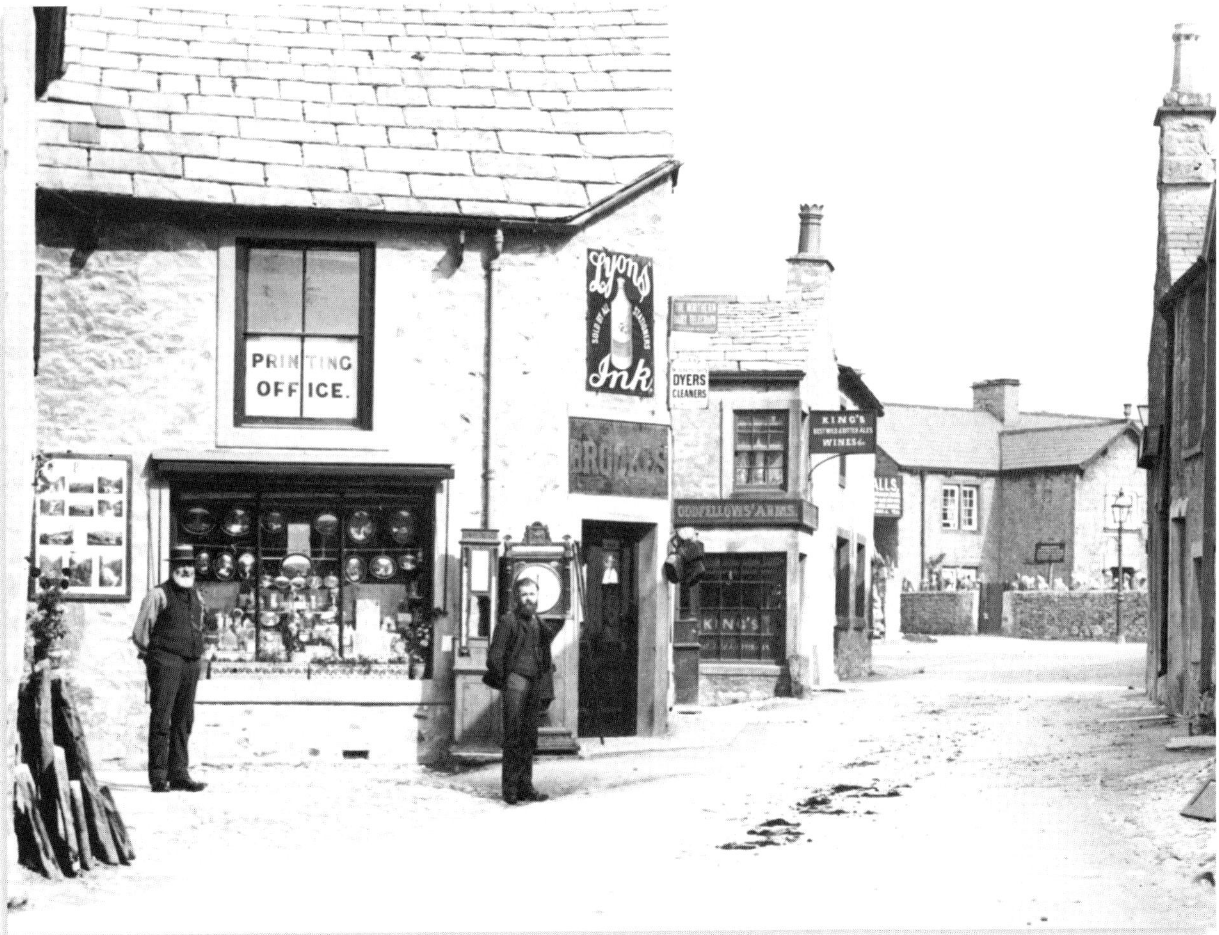

FROM THE AIR

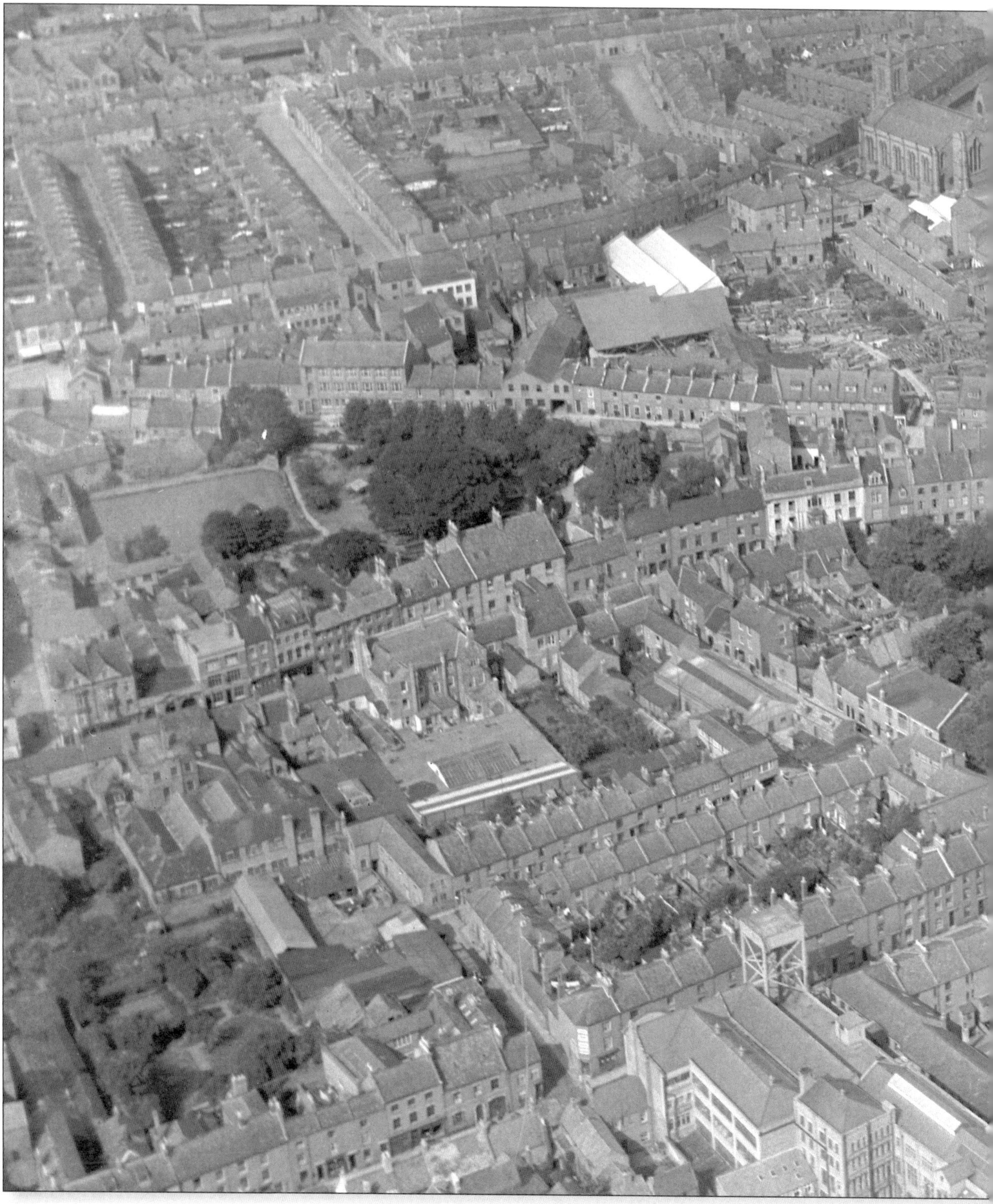

From The Air

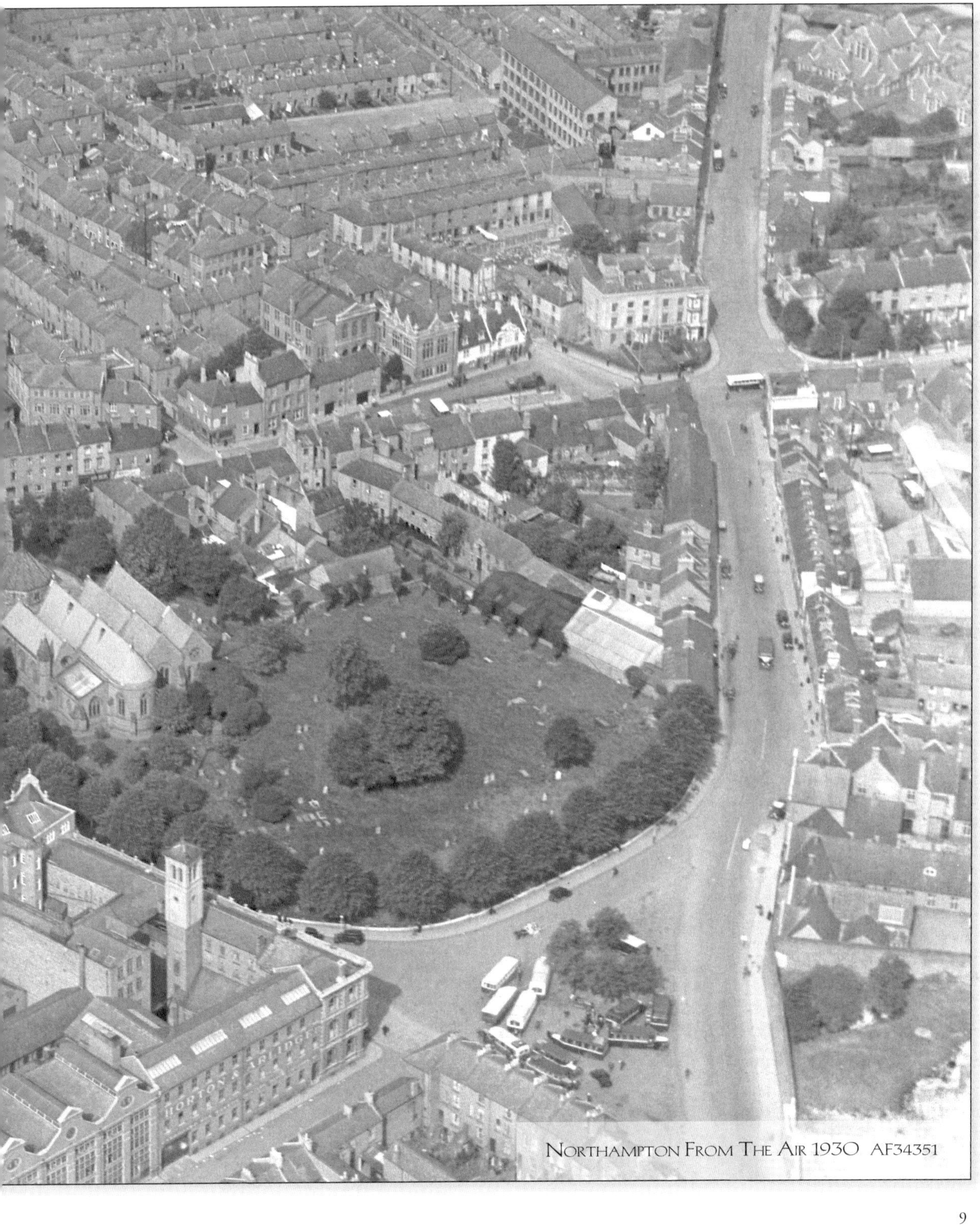

Northampton From The Air 1930 AF34351

FROM THE DANELAW TO NORTHAMPTON

"Simon de St Liz received it (Northampton) from William the Conqueror, took from it the title of Earl, fortified it with walls and a castle, and speedily raised it to comparatively high prosperity. It soon became the occasional residence of several of the kings, and acquired for a time a quasi-metro-political influence."

BRABNER'S GAZETTEER OF ENGLAND AND WALES 1895

"The town stands on a gentle ascent, on the left bank of the Nen (Nene), and has charming environs, adorned with wood and gemmed with mansions and villas."

The description is still recognisable, despite the accretions of a greatly-expanded modern industrial town, the county town of Northamptonshire. The River Nene flowing in its wide, flat valley south and west of the town, and the extensive areas of parkland, such as Becketts Park, Delapre Park to the south of the river, Abington Park to the east of the town and Race Course Recreation Ground to its north-east, help to conserve much of the historic town's character.

The town has expanded west and south of the Nene, and even further east and north-east to absorb several villages within its maw: Duston, Dallington, Kingsthorpe, Abington, Great and Little Billing and Weston Favell, for example. This book visits two of them: one, Abington, is outstandingly interesting, and one, Duston, is less so, but it concentrates mainly on the core of historic Northampton, a town with a long and distinguished history. A royal town in the Middle Ages, it was staunchly pro-Parliament in the 17th-century Civil War. This chapter looks briefly at a fascinating era that has left relatively few buildings standing from before 1675, when a catastrophic fire consumed the heart of the town.

There was nothing much here until the Danish conquests, when it became an important military and administrative town ruled by the Danes from AD877 to 918. Reconquered by Edward the Elder, he made it the centre of one of his new 'shires' or counties; it prospered as a river port and trading centre, despite being burnt in 1010 by Thorkil and a Danish army, and again in 1065 by the rebellious northern earls Edwin and Morcar.

The town's physical situation, where the River Nene cuts through the limestone ridge and turns northwards along its west edge, provided an ideal defensive location, as well as the control over a major river crossing where key routes converged from all directions. After the Norman Conquest, and by the time of Domesday Book in 1087, the town had 316 merchants' houses, and the strategic value of the town, virtually in the centre of the kingdom, was recognised by the building of a castle. This was undertaken by the town's Norman overlord, Simon de Senlis or St Lis, about 1086. It was probably originally an earth and timber stockaded construction, which was rebuilt in stone over the next two centuries. We will search in vain for this castle, for it suffered two cruel fates, the first after the Civil War and the Commonwealth, for in 1662 Charles II, restored to his throne, took vengeance on the pro-Parliamentarian town by ordering the castle to be slighted or demolished. A fair amount survived this indignity, only to succumb in the 19th century when the railway station was built across its site in 1879.

A plaque commemorates the castle in Chalk Lane, which runs curving north along the course of the castle's eastern moat from Mare Fair and away from one of Northampton's most striking medieval churches, St Peter's. From the river and the castle the medieval town ran eastwards, with the Market Square as its focus. The medieval town walls, demolished as well as the castle at the orders of Charles II in 1662, enclosed about 245 acres (98 hectares), with St Giles's Church near the east gate and Holy Sepulchre towards the north gate. All Saints', near the market place and in the centre of the town, is also medieval in part, but it was mostly rebuilt after the 1675 fire.

From the pre-fire period three major medieval parish churches survive, two of outstanding interest, Holy Sepulchre and St Peter's. Holy Sepulchre, in the north of the walled town, has a circular nave (72198, page 14) whose plan copies that of the church of the Holy Sepulchre in Jerusalem; it is a direct link with the Crusades, when the Holy Land was conquered by western European knights. Simon de Senlis, Earl of Northampton, had himself been a crusader, and founded this most unusual church upon his return from Palestine before 1112: there are very few round churches in England.

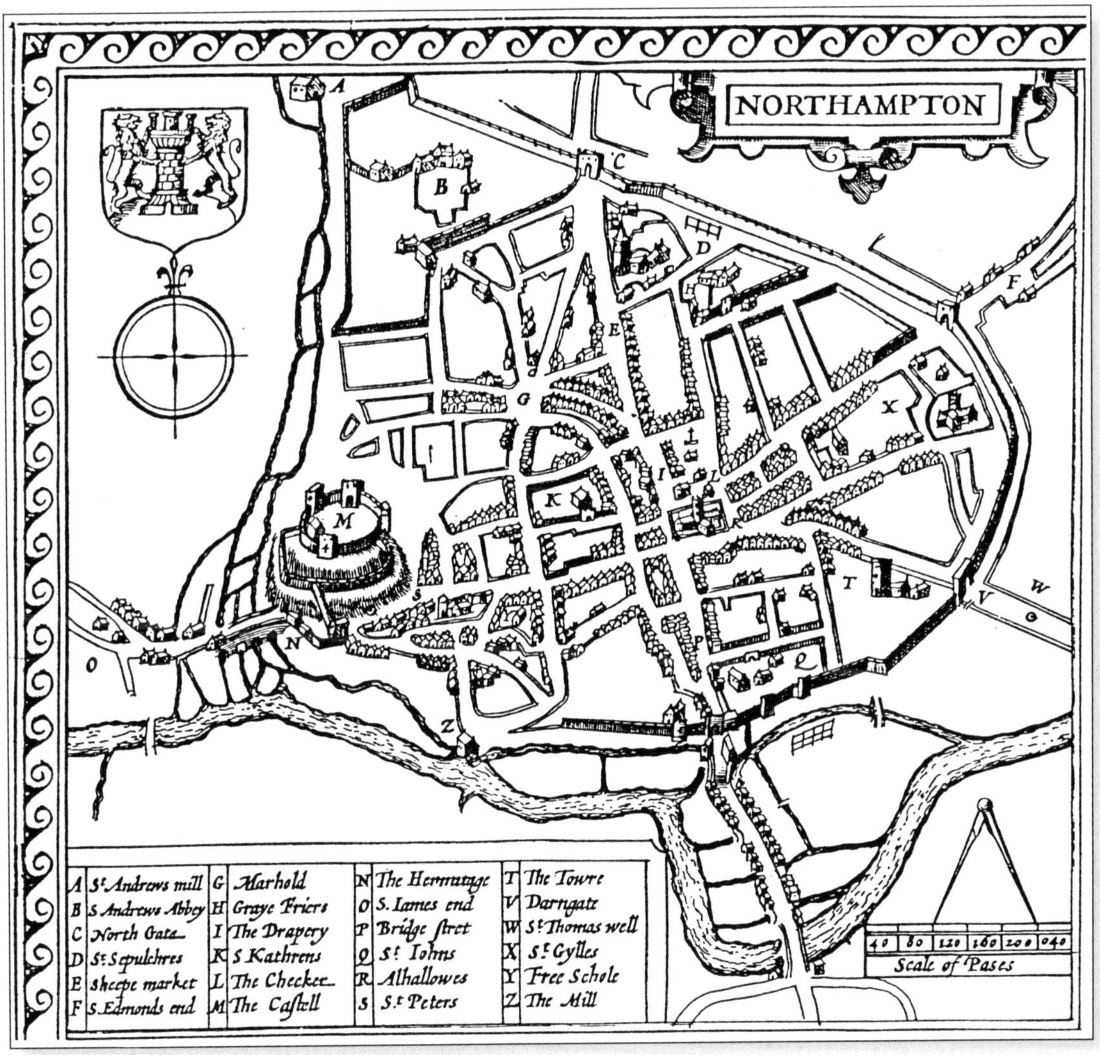

JOHN SPEED'S VIEW OF NORTHAMPTON IN 1610
(REPRODUCED BY KIND PERMISSION OF NORTHAMPTON CENTRAL LIBRARY)

Equally astonishing, this time for its sculptural richness, is St Peter's, near the castle site (72200, pages 17); it dates from around 1170 and is built in late Norman ornate style. St Giles's, at the east end of town, has a Norman crossing tower with the rest later medieval; but All Saints' in the centre (72191, page 29) retains only its medieval tower and chancel crypt.

Besides these medieval parish churches, there were various monasteries and friaries in Northampton, as befitted a major town with royal connections — the castle had been taken over by the king around 1130. These included a wealthy Cluniac monastery, St Andrew's Priory, founded by Simon de Senlis around 1100. Although it is long gone, it is commemorated in the names St Andrew's Street, off Broad Street, and Priory Street. There was also a house of Augustinian canons, St James' Abbey, which stood west of the river, and is commemorated by St James's Street. There were three friaries: a Franciscan friary founded in 1226, now remembered by Greyfriars Street near the bus station; Blackfriars, founded around 1230 and sited near Horse Market; and Whitefriars, founded in 1265, which stood near Wood Street. Also there was a medieval hospital, St John's (its use was in fact closer to an almshouse than a modern hospital), founded by William de St Clare about 1138. This actually survives in part, and is situated east of Bridge Street. Bought in 1877 for a Roman Catholic community, in 1955 the almshouses were converted into a church and the medieval chapel became a side chapel to this church.

Apparently Richard I granted the town its own coinage mint, and it accumulated several fairs and market charters. Northampton stayed within its walls until the 19th century, apart from suburbs outside the south, west and north-east gates. These were along South Quarter between the town wall and the River Nene, now part of Bridge Street, St James End beyond the west gate which grew up around the Augustinian abbey, and St Edmunds End, now the area around present-day Abington Square.

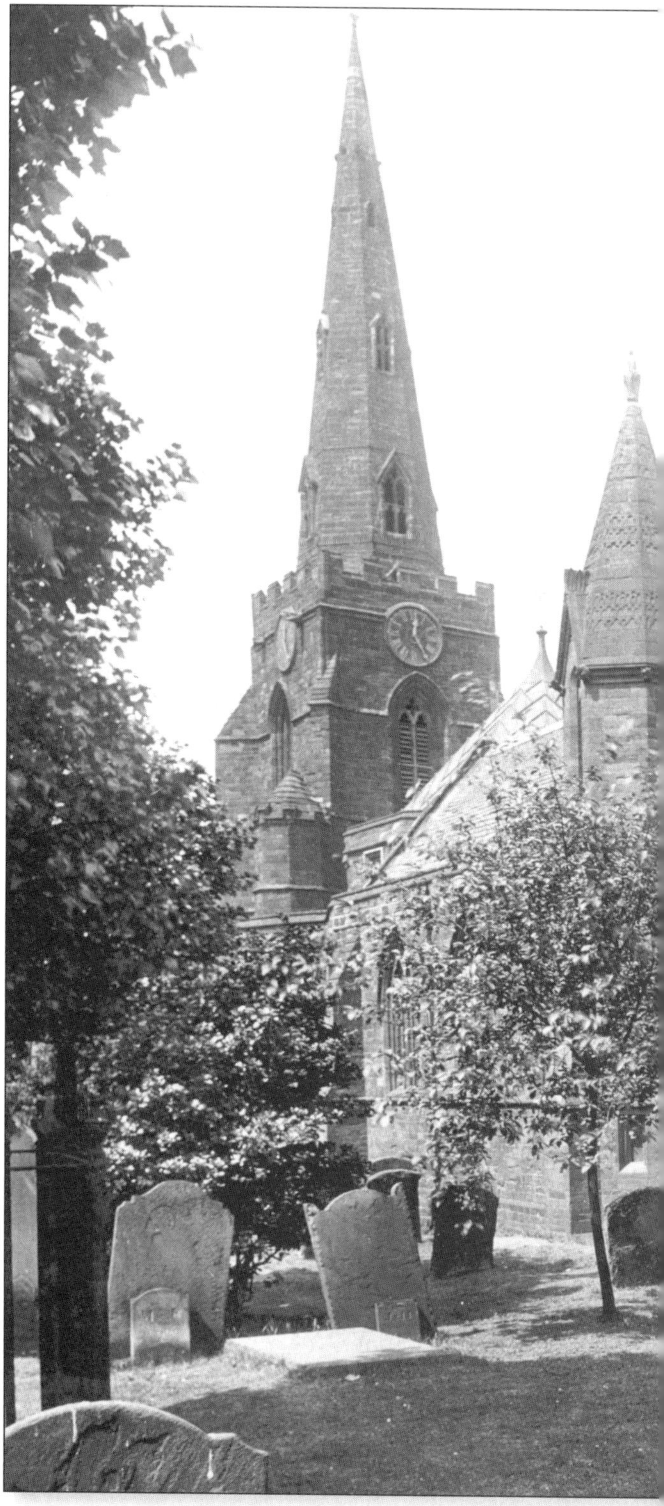

THE CHURCH OF THE HOLY SEPULCHRE 1922 72195

This remarkable church with its circular nave dates from the early 12th century. Founded by Simon de Senlis, the crusader Earl of Northampton, soon after 1100 upon his return from the Holy Land, it is based on the plan of the church of the Holy Sepulchre in Jerusalem. This nave is next to the tower, but the church was enlarged with a fine 13th-century chancel and later chapels to its east, and a 14th-century tower and spire added to its west. The views on these and the following pages show the round nave inside and two exterior views of the mellow golden-brown ironstone church, one through the fine 1877 lych-gate.

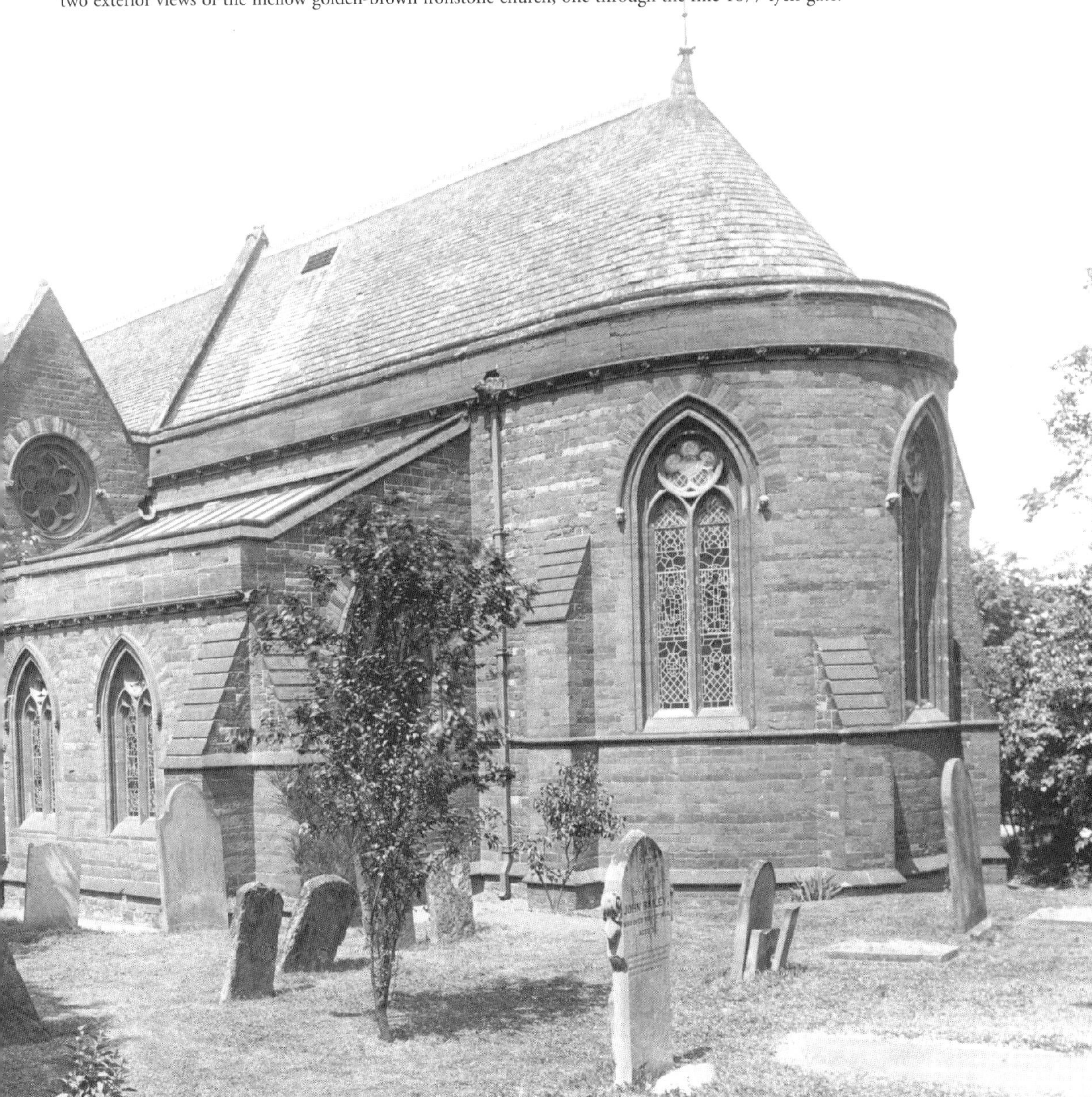

"The parish church (All Saints) stands nearly in the centre of the town, and must have been a magnificent structure – cruciform in shape, with the tower rising from the intersection; the nave reached half-way across the drapery."

BRABNER'S GAZETTEER OF ENGLAND AND WALES 1895

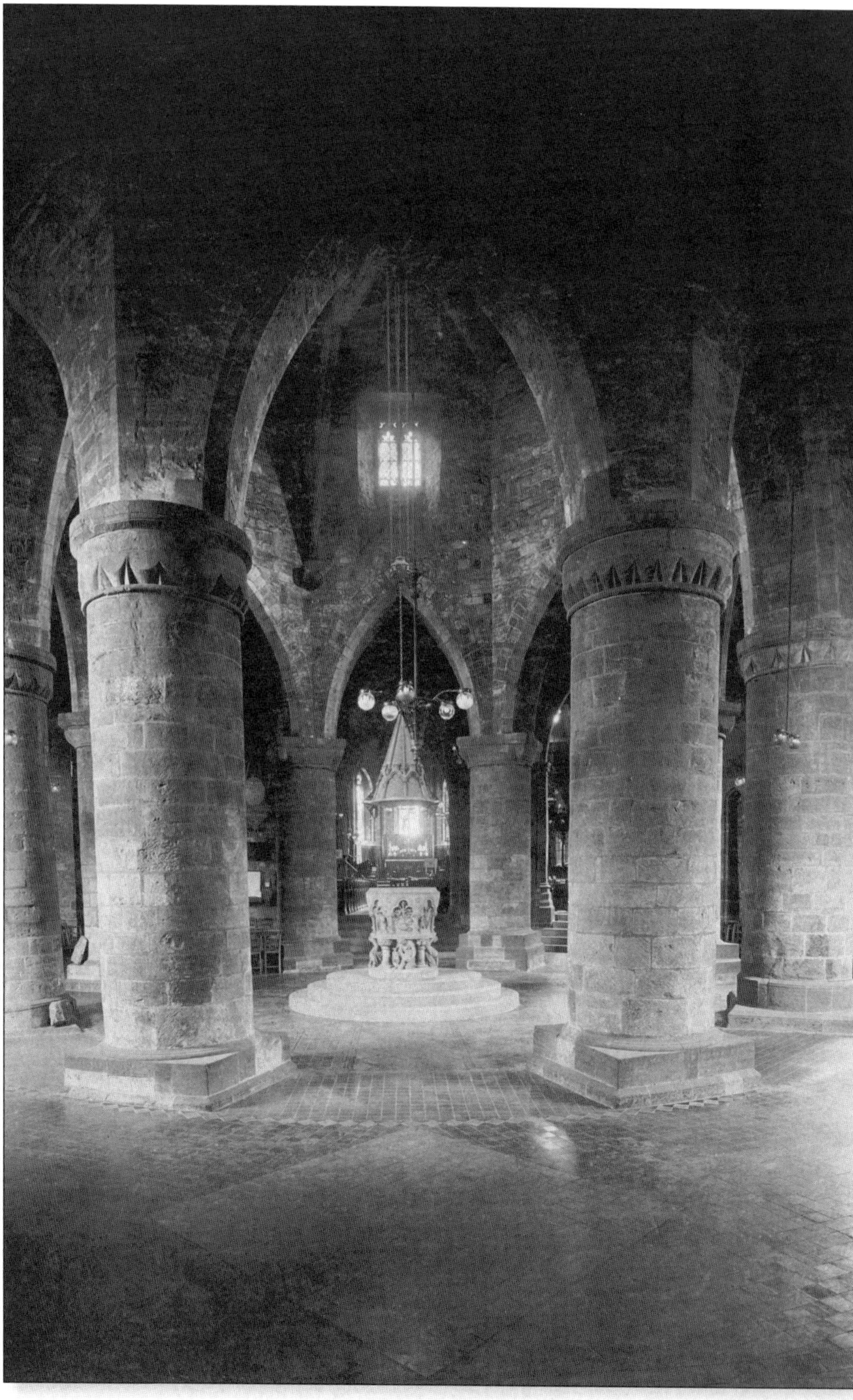

THE CHURCH OF THE HOLY SEPULCHRE 1922 72198

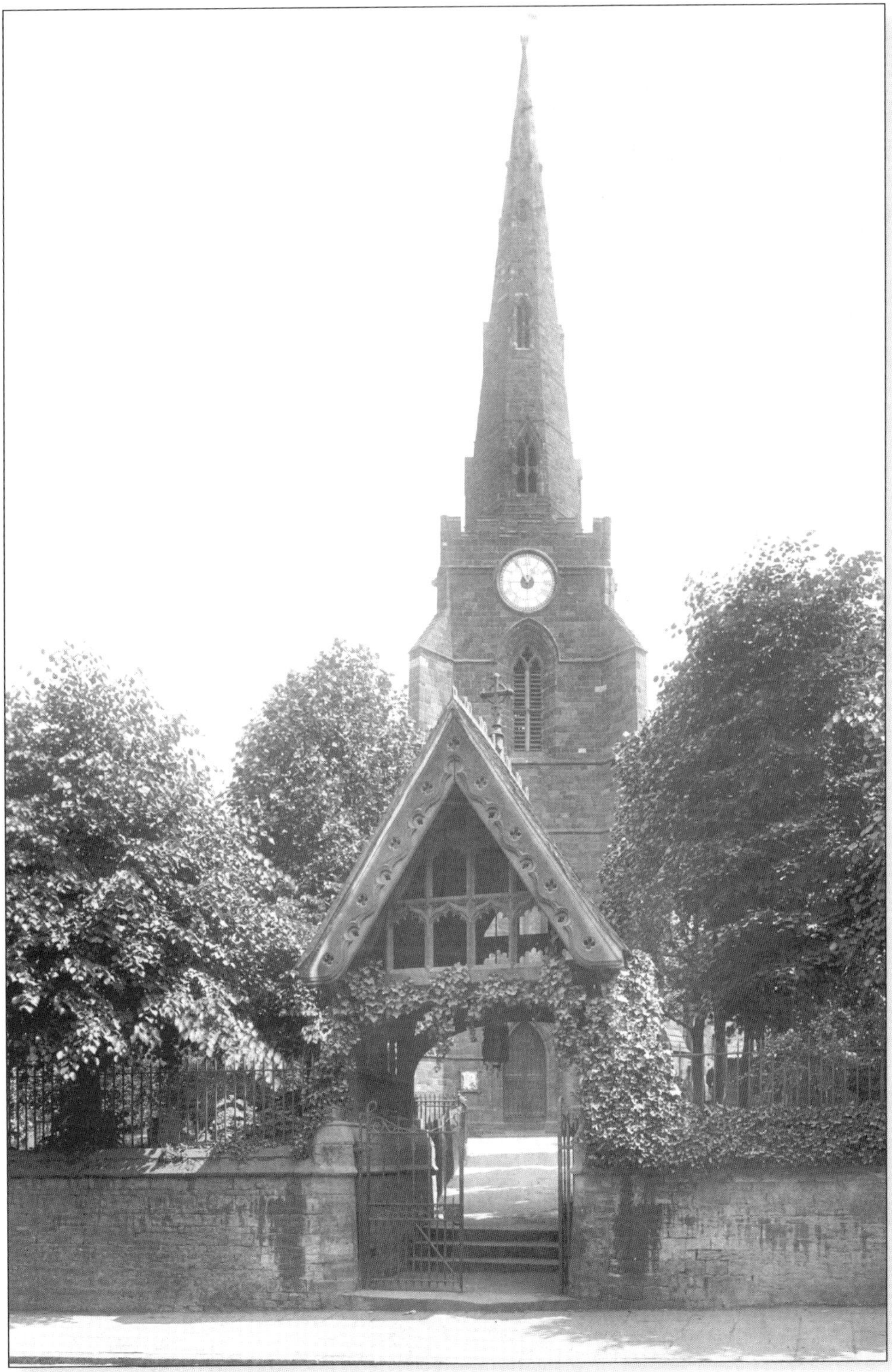

THE CHURCH OF THE HOLY SEPULCHRE 1922 72196

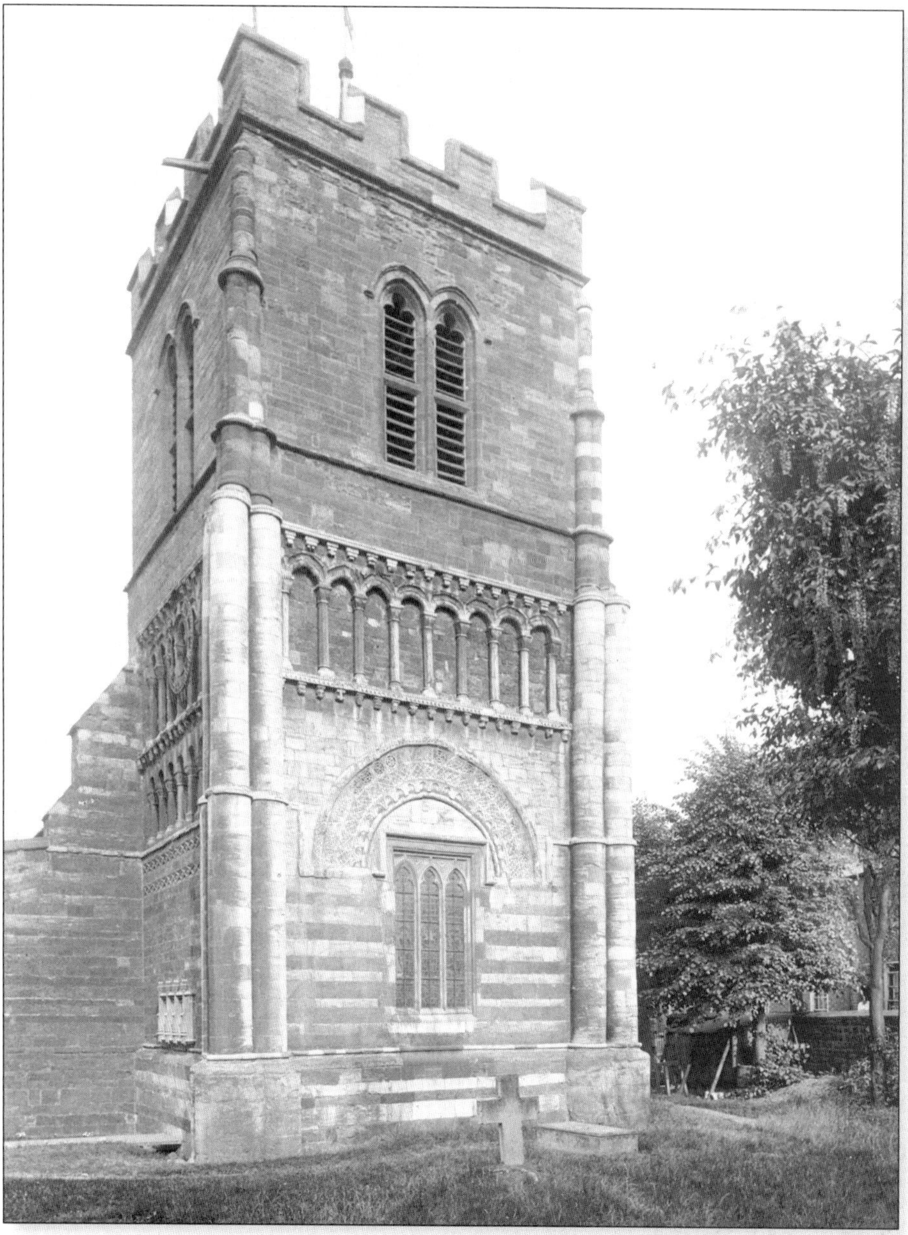

ST PETER'S CHURCH, THE NORMAN TOWER 72201

St Peter's Church, immediately south of the site of Simon de Senlis's Norman castle (by this time in royal hands), was rebuilt around 1160 to 1170 by his grandson, another Simon. The church was built in the exuberantly decorated Late Norman style, and the views on these pages depict some of the profuse carved ornament on the arches and capitals.

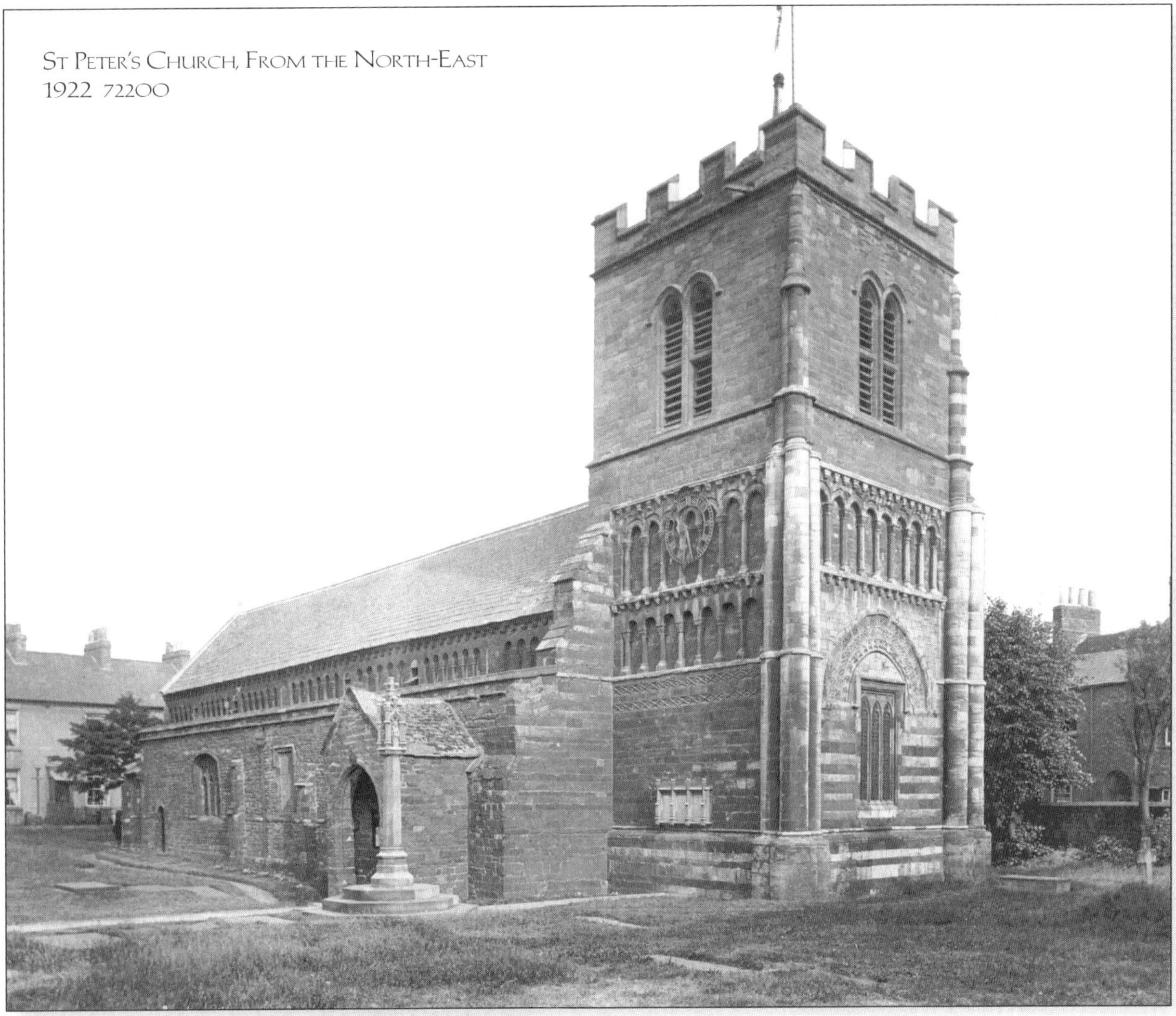

ST PETER'S CHURCH, FROM THE NORTH-EAST
1922 72200

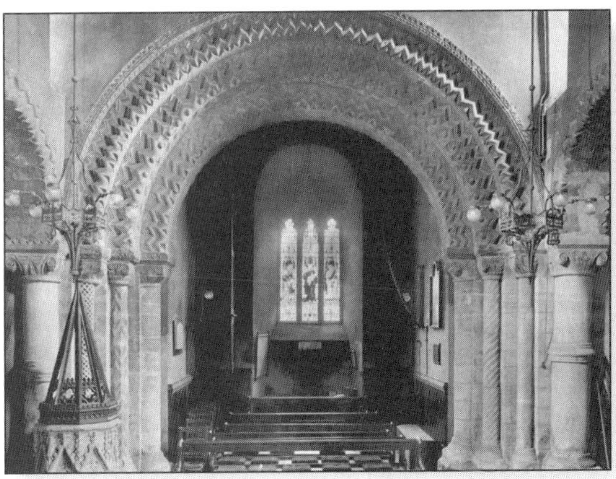

Left:
ST PETER'S CHURCH, THE INTERIOR LOOKING WEST 1922
72203

The carving exudes an almost barbaric air: the capitals are full of curious foliage inhabited by mythical winged creatures, writhing figures and animals, and the arches are a profusion of geometric decoration — a marked contrast to the more chaste Gothic style just then emerging from France. The tower was rebuilt in the 17th century, apart from the arch into the nave we see in this view of the interior.

FROM THE DANELAW TO

Northampton, its castle an occasional royal residence, witnessed many important events as the Middle Ages unfolded. It held both the forerunner of parliament (which was more of a great royal council) and full parliaments, before these finally settled in the royal palace of Westminster after following the king around the country. The royal council first met in the town from Stephen's reign, and during Henry II's reign Northampton was host to the council that arraigned Thomas à Beckett, the Archbishop of Canterbury and Henry's one-time friend and chancellor. Thomas à Beckett was a great disappointment to the king, who had hoped that he would be a willing ally in bringing the church under royal control. He was wrong, and Beckett was arraigned in Northampton Castle in 1164. The first parliament attended by burgesses or merchants, the forerunners of the later House of Commons, was held at Northampton in 1179. After the Barons' Wars of the 1260s, when the town was besieged and captured from Simon de Montfort, the barons' leader, several parliaments were held here, including the notorious one of 1380 when the first poll tax was passed. This hated measure provoked the Peasants' Revolt the following year.

Besides the more formal elements of medieval governance, there were great royal entertainments in Northampton. For instance, King Stephen held a feast at Easter 1122, and tournaments or jousts were very popular, including one in 1241 when Peter de Savoy, the Queen's uncle, tilted.

However, in the 15th century the royal connection became less significant, and by the time of the Civil War in the 1640s Northampton was decidedly pro-Parliament. The town had a long history of religious dissent from the Lollards of the early 15th century onwards, and Puritanism gained a strong hold on the town. The corporation, having already refused to provide troops to the King in 1632 or to pay the notorious Ship Money tax in 1636, petitioned Parliament in 1642 against papists and bishops.

When the Civil War started, the town willingly became one of the most important Parliamentary garrison towns; it eagerly set about improving the defences, using the former royal castle as garrison headquarters. Oliver Cromwell visited in 1645, and General Fairfax marched from the town to Naseby, where Charles I's Royalist army was decisively defeated. An interesting sidelight and pointer to Northampton's later fame was the manufacture of over 4,000 pairs of leather shoes and 600 pairs of cavalry jack-boots for the Parliamentary armies during the Civil War, and a further 2,000 for Cromwell's New Model Army in 1648.

However, after the Commonwealth, England's sole dalliance with a republic, the town corporation's attempts to mend fences with the restored Charles II failed; in 1662 he took revenge, not only by having the town walls and the now tainted castle demolished, but also by purging the corporation. The new council had to pay £200 to have its charter renewed. This revised document required all officials to swear the oath of allegiance, and several office-holders had to have their positions confirmed by the Crown.

Nature, however, soon intervened to effect a reconciliation: the Great Fire of 1675 restored harmony — indeed, Charles II donated timber from the nearby royal forests for the rebuilding. The fire, which started in a thatched cottage in St Mary's Street, was spread eastwards by strong westerly winds, described by the then Town Clerk thus: 'The wind was very strong to blow ye fire on, but it was God who blew ye bellows'. The fire consumed three-quarters of the town, including Horsefair, the Market Place and Abington Street. Very little survived the fire, apart from the stone churches and a couple of stone-built houses. One is the Welsh House of 1595 in Market Place, now restored to its original appearance with its elaborate gabled dormers, and the other is Hazelrigg House in Mare Fair (page 22-23), which was south-west of the fire and in an area largely untouched by it. This was built in 1662, and also has high stone gabled dormers.

The next chapter takes the story of Northampton on from the rebuilding after the 1675 Fire into the age of photography, although Frith's intrepid cameramen did not reach the town until the 1920s, which are covered in Chapter 3.

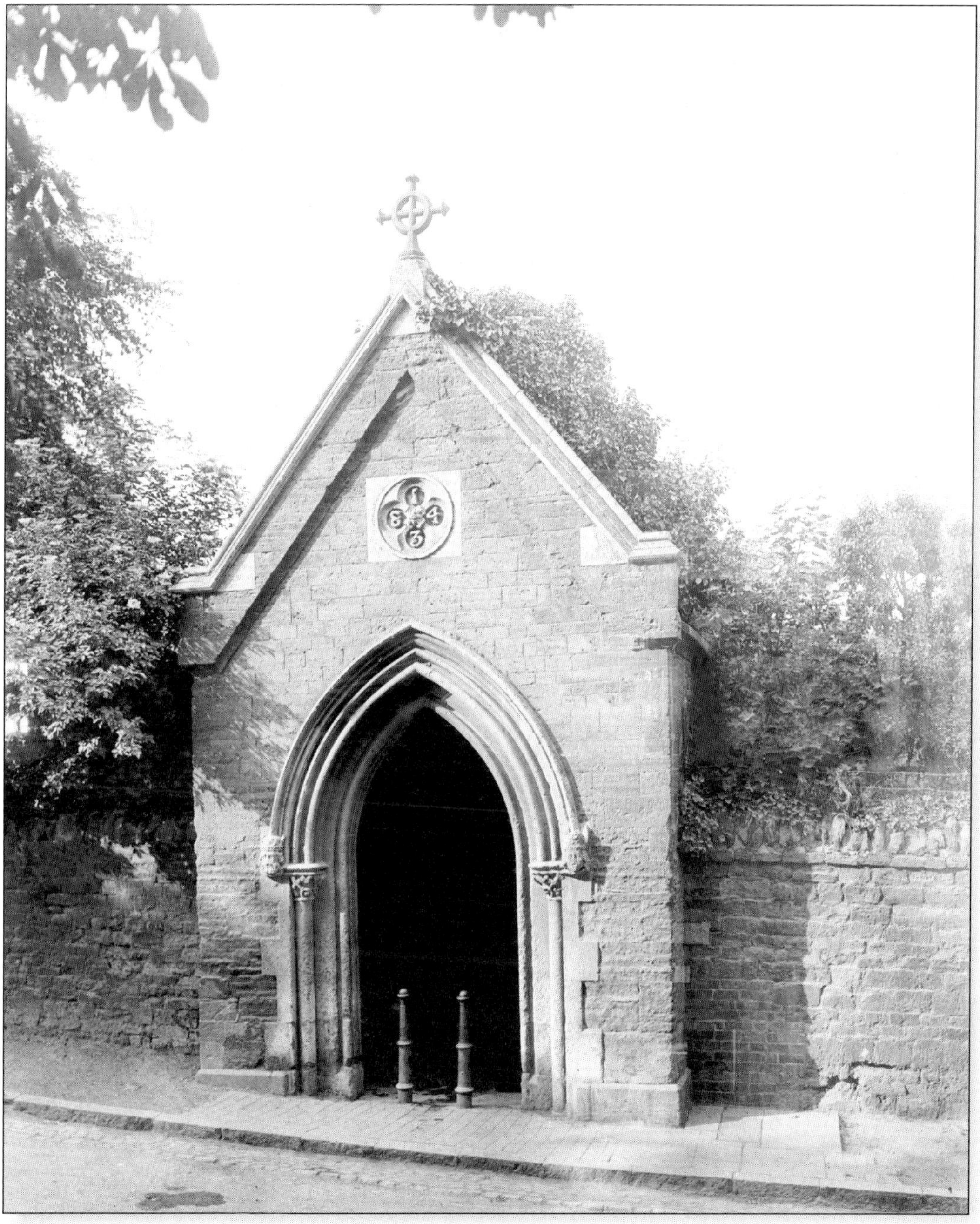

THE THOMAS A BECKETT WELL 1922 72190

After his trial for treason at Northampton in 1164, Thomas à Beckett escaped from St Andrew's Priory. By an ancient tradition he is supposed to have stopped at a well on the Bedford Road for a drink before continuing on his way, eventually taking ship for France and exile. He returned to England, of course, and was martyred in Canterbury Cathedral in 1170. The well, marked on the 1610 John Speed map, had its well-house rebuilt by the corporation in 1843 in Gothic style.

FROM THE DANELAW TO

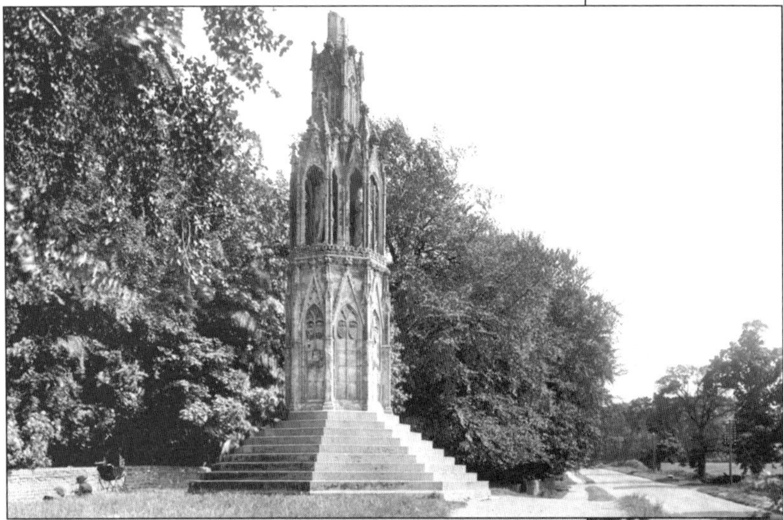

Above: THE QUEEN ELEANOR CROSS 1922 72188

When Edward I's beloved wife Eleanor of Castile died in November 1290, the distraught king had elaborate crosses erected where her coffin rested overnight on its way from Nottinghamshire to Charing Cross in London. These elaborate structures copied what the French had done for their king Louis IX in 1271. Three of them survive, and this one was built in 1291 by John of Battle with statues carved by William of Ireland.

"A fire consumed 600 houses and one of the churches in 1675. The desolation ... affected the greater part of the town, made an easy prey of the houses in consequence of their being chiefly built of wood and covered with thatch, and destroyed property estimated at £150,000 in value, but it led to the obtaining an Act of Parliament for rebuilding the town, and occasioned it to be transformed from a state of meanness to a state of comparative beauty."

BRABNER'S GAZETTEER OF ENGLAND AND WALES 1895

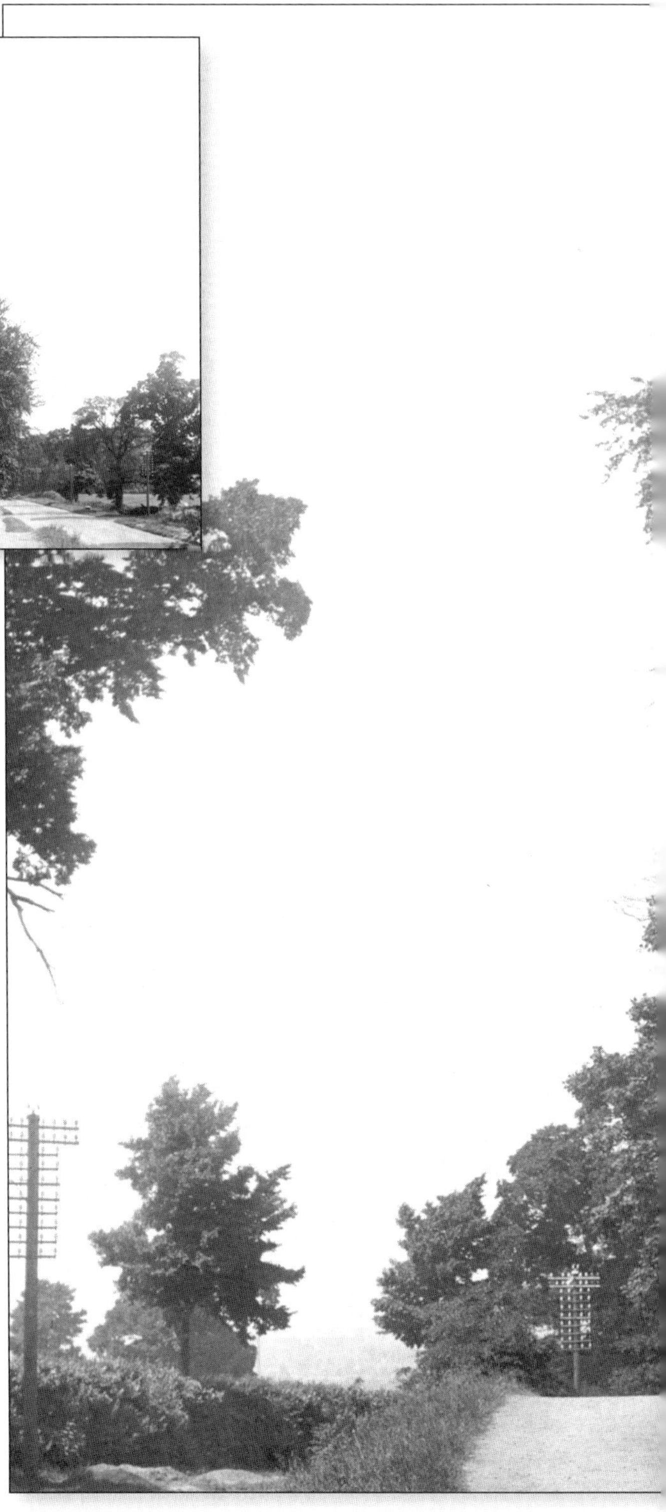

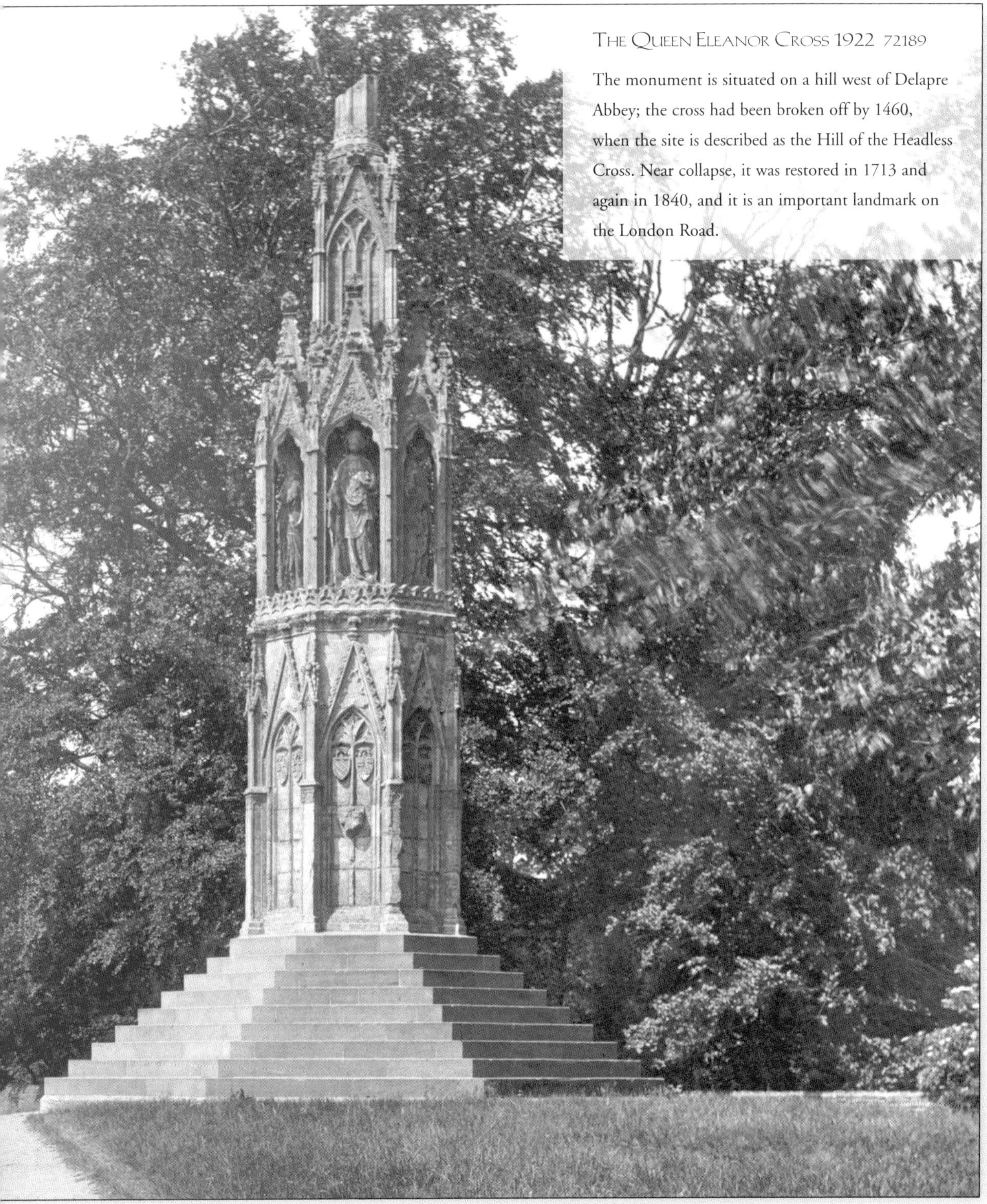

THE QUEEN ELEANOR CROSS 1922 72189

The monument is situated on a hill west of Delapre Abbey; the cross had been broken off by 1460, when the site is described as the Hill of the Headless Cross. Near collapse, it was restored in 1713 and again in 1840, and it is an important landmark on the London Road.

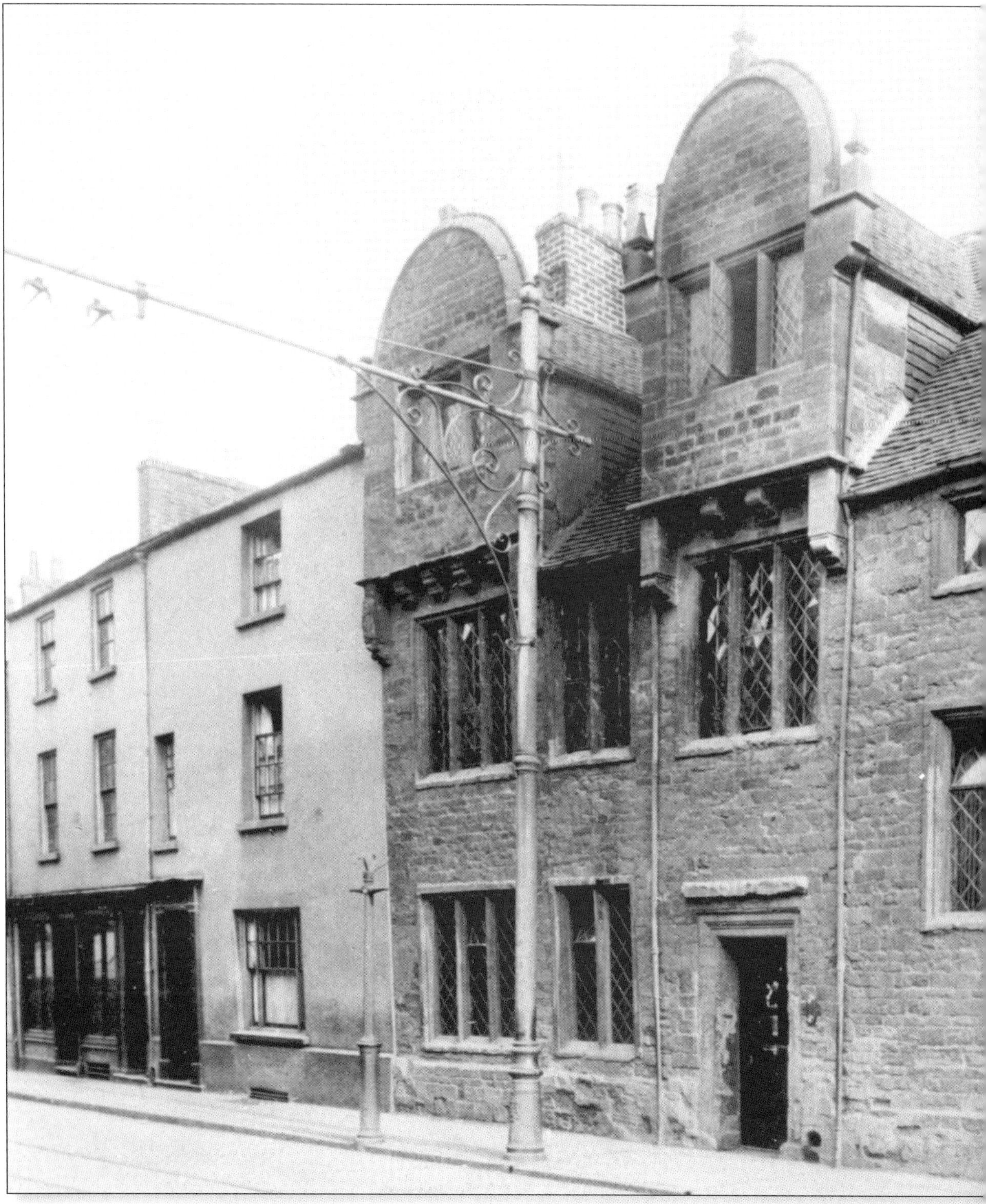

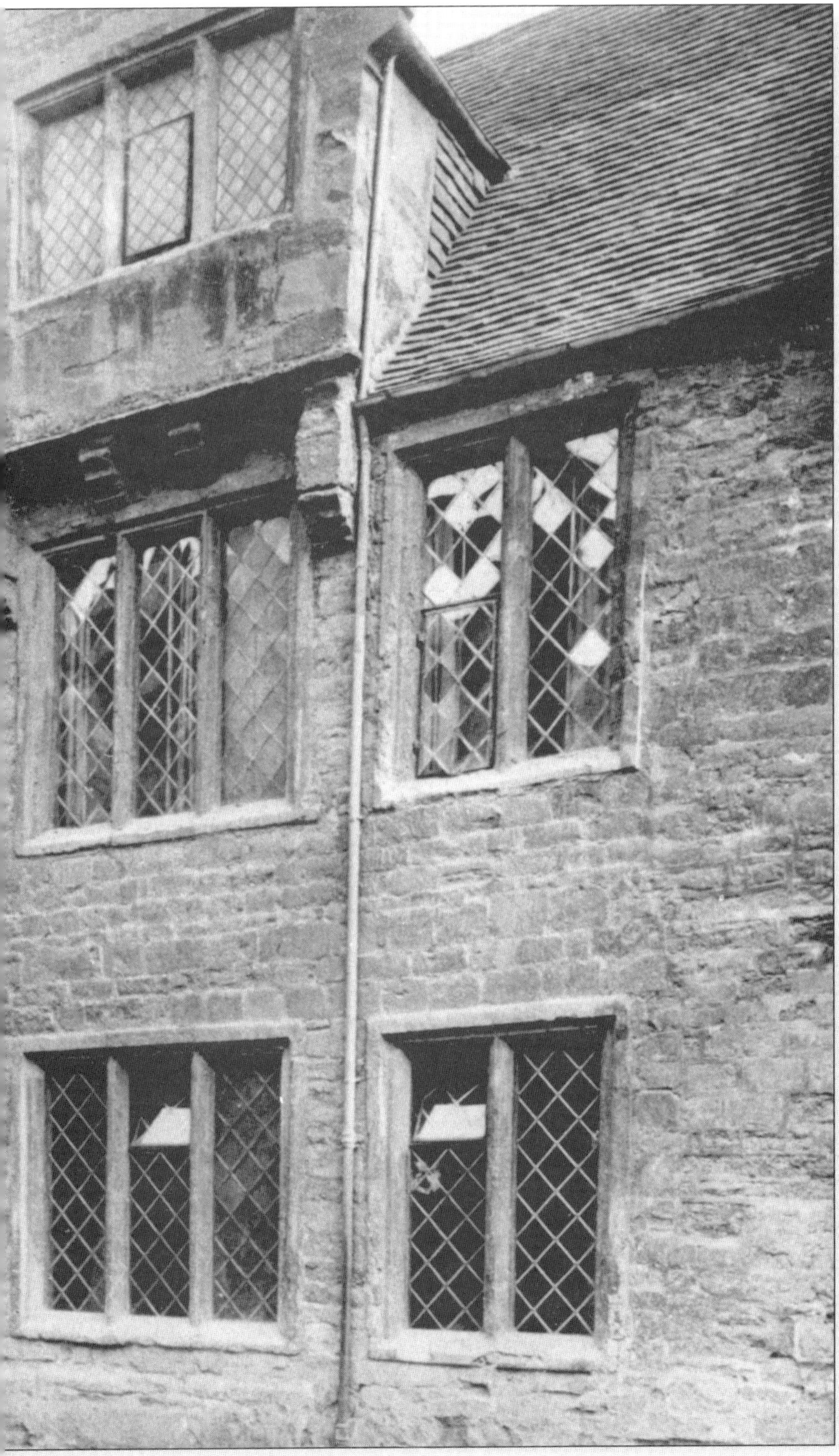

HAZELRIGG HOUSE OR CROMWELL HOUSE, MARE FAIR 1922 72177

Hazelrigg House, on Mare Fair at the west end of town, escaped the fire, which was fanned by strong westerly winds towards the market place. Apparently built in 1662, it was bought by Robert Hazelrigg in 1678, and remained in the family until 1835. The legend of Oliver Cromwell spending the night here before Naseby is romantic but fanciful. Now with three round gabled dormers, the house was originally two bays longer; but it is a fine reminder of the town before the 1675 fire, and is one of only two or three domestic survivors of the disaster.

NORTHAMPTON

County Map

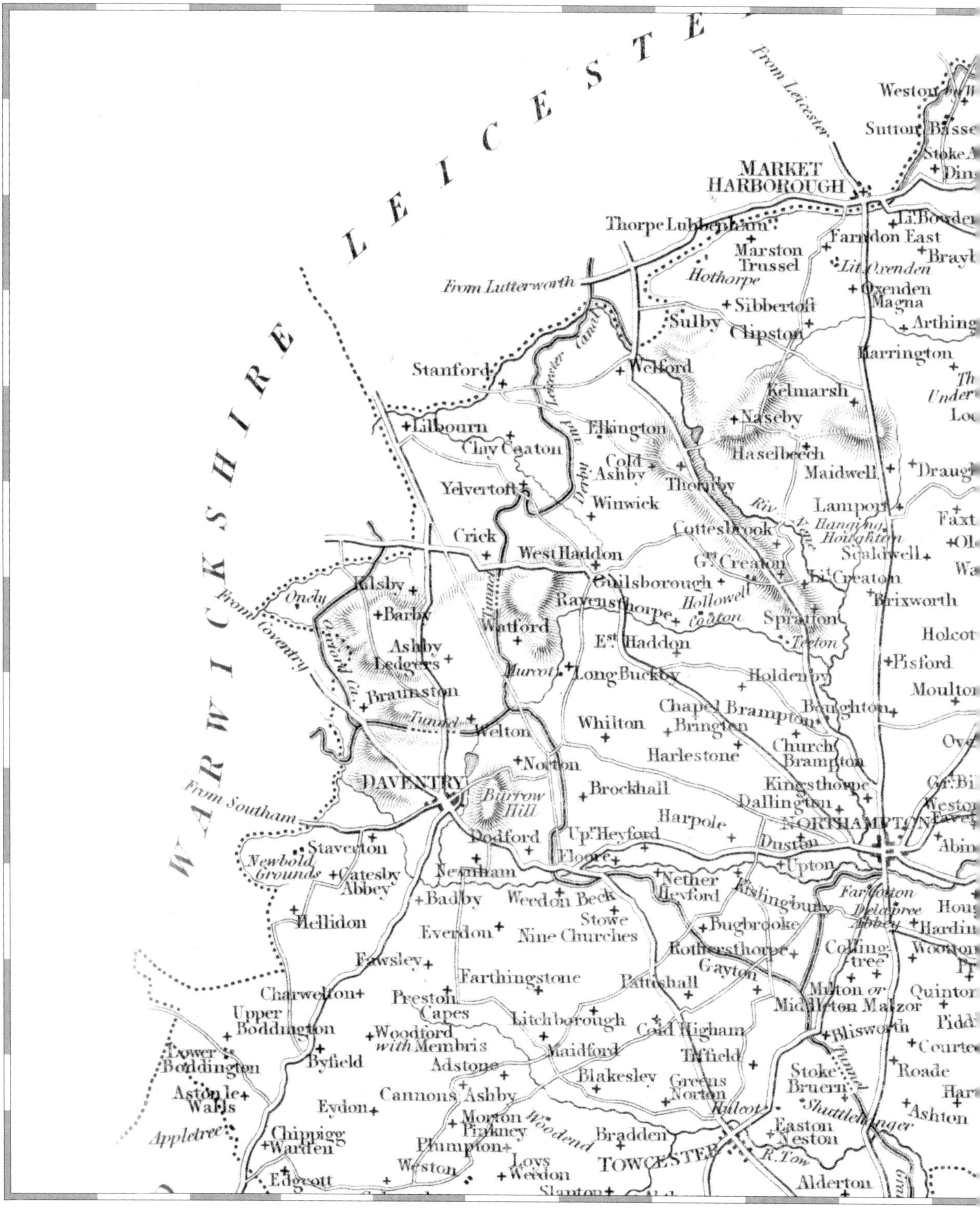

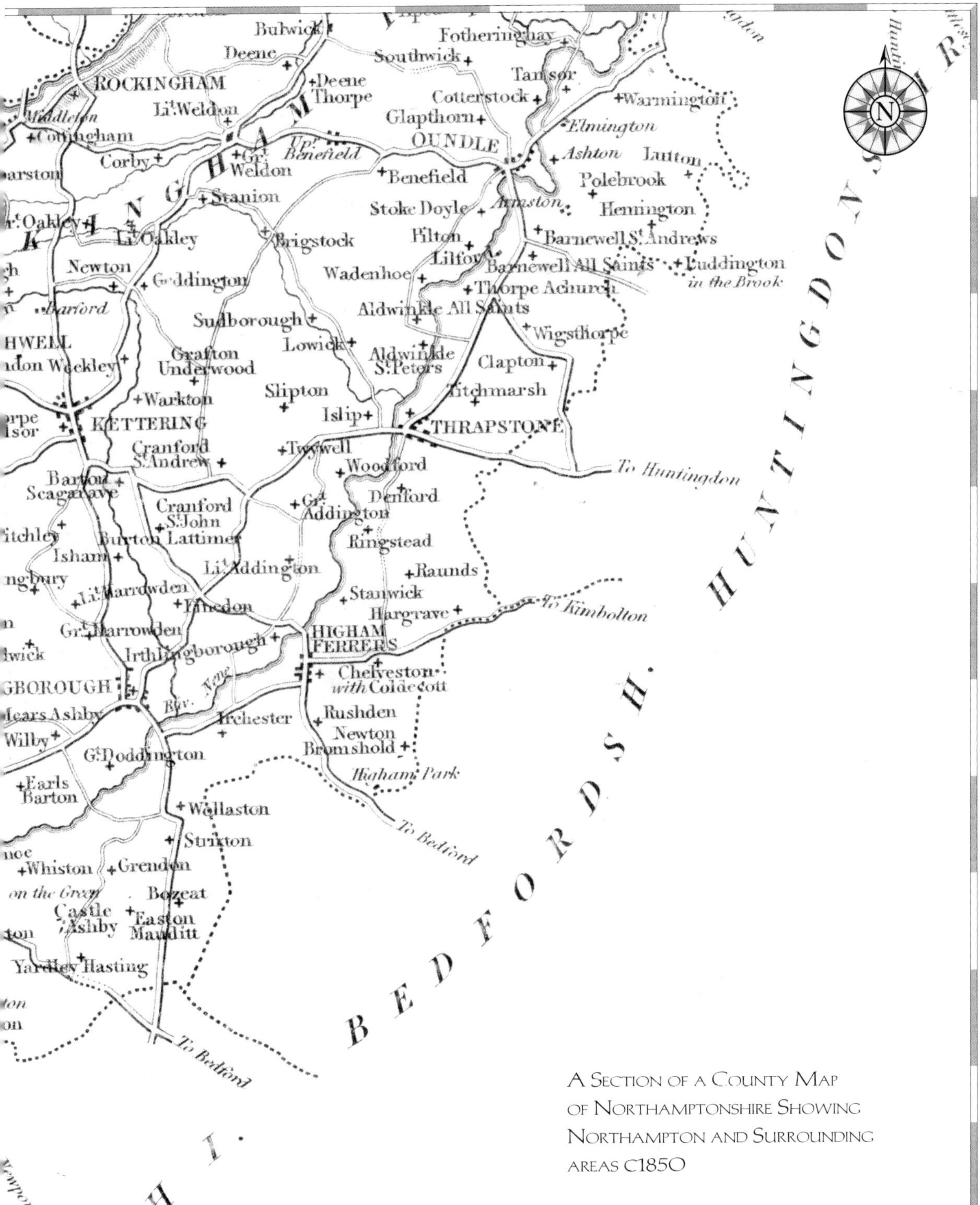

A SECTION OF A COUNTY MAP OF NORTHAMPTONSHIRE SHOWING NORTHAMPTON AND SURROUNDING AREAS C1850

FROM THE 1675 FIRE

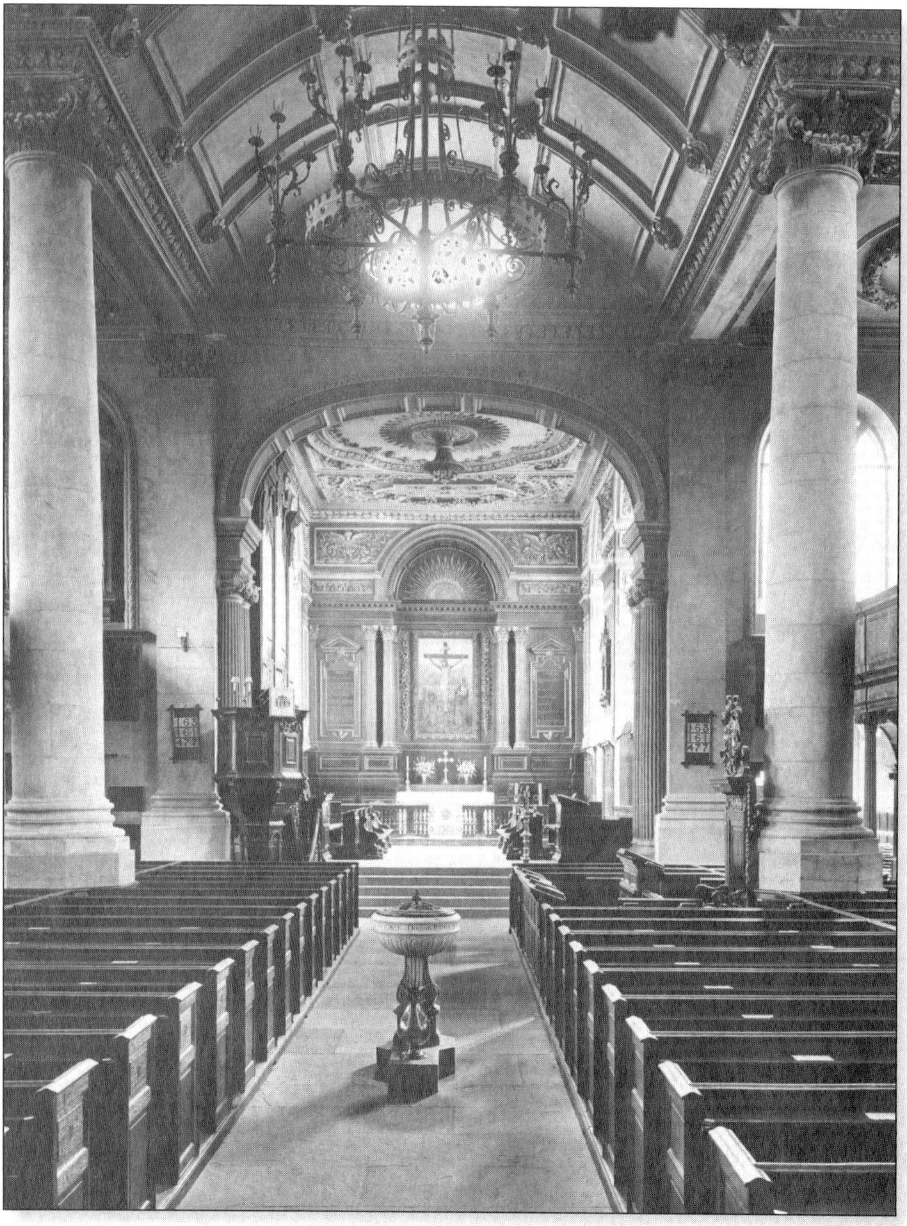

ALL SAINTS' CHURCH, THE INTERIOR LOOKING EAST 1922 72191A

BRABNER'S GAZETTEER OF ENGLAND AND WALES 1895

"All Saints ... all except the Early English tower (which is burnt red in places) was destroyed by a fire in 1675. The work of rebuilding was at once commenced in accordance with the then popular classical style, and in 1680 the church was re-opened for worship. King Charles II gave a thousand tons of timber towards the rebuilding, and his gift is commemorated by an inscription along the portico and his statue in Roman costume above."

Rebuilt after the 1675 fire, this classical-style church was designed by Henry Bell from King's Lynn and completed in 1680. The medieval tower, originally a crossing tower, was retained, and a forecourt or square was created in front of the portico on the site of the medieval nave. The cupola on the tower was added in 1704, and the statue of Charles II was set above the portico in 1712 in belated gratitude for the king's help in the rebuilding.

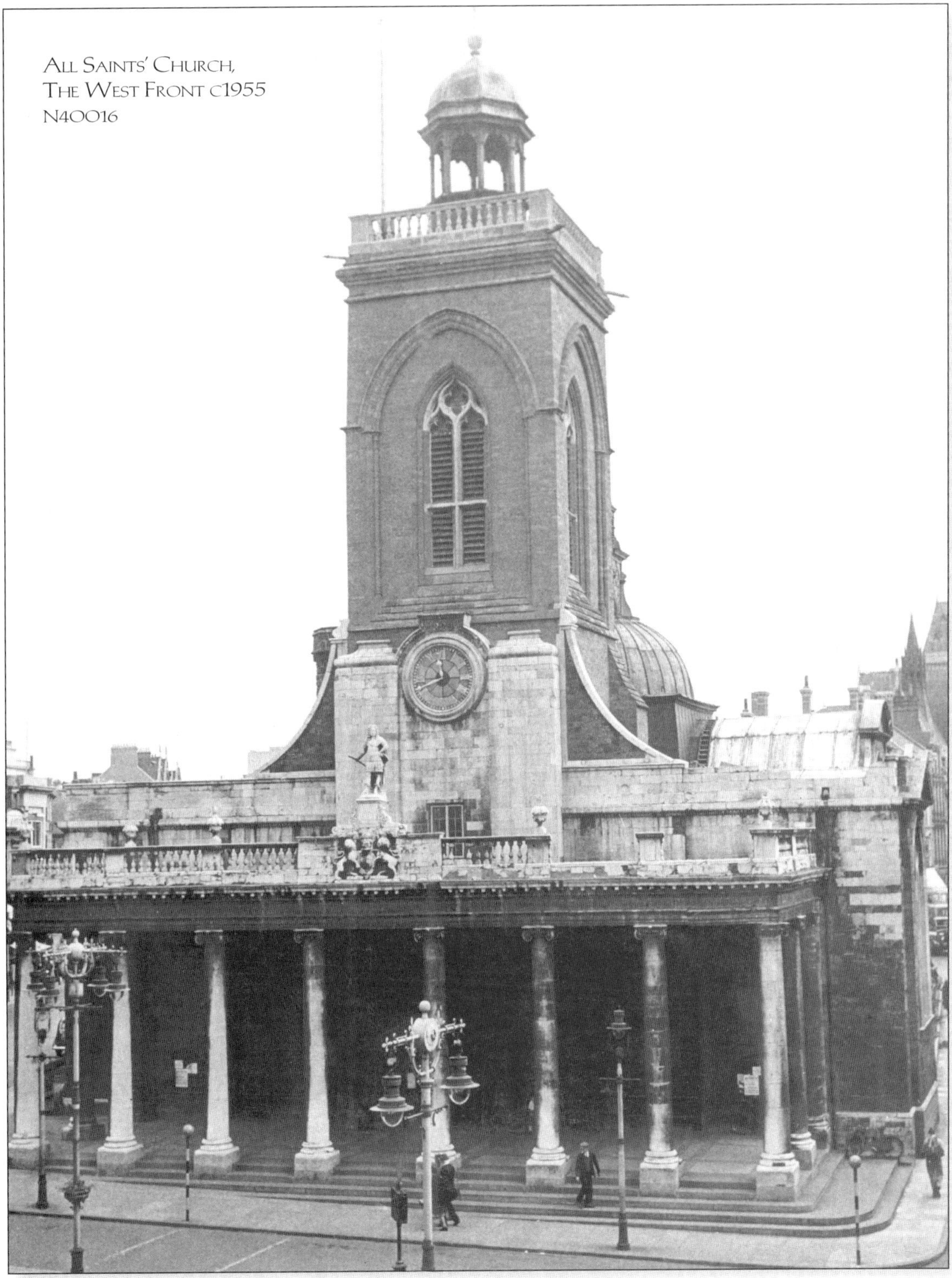

ALL SAINTS' CHURCH, THE WEST FRONT c1955 N40016

FROM THE 1675 FIRE

One of the first buildings reconstructed after the devastating fire of September 1675 was the main parish church of All Saints, its 14th-century tower with 1617 repairs incorporated in the new work. Although Barber's 'Gazetteer' attributes the work to Christopher Wren, it was probably designed by Henry Bell, the architect of King's Lynn's famous Customs House. The rebuilding of the town was authorised by an Act of Parliament later in the same year of 1675, its speed a reflection of the Recorder, the then Earl of Northampton, and the local merchants and gentry's urgent desire to get the town back on its feet. Besides the cost being raised by public subscription, the hearth or chimney tax was put towards the work of the rebuilding Commissioners.

Rather like London after its Great Fire in 1666, the opportunity for radical re-planning of the streets with squares and wider roads was largely ignored, so the town arose on a similar street plan to before — but not surprisingly without timber-framed houses and thatched roofs. All Saints' was the grandest building, although it was shorter than before; in a way it was a symbol of the revived town. Indeed, ten per cent of the rebuilding money went to its reconstruction. All around the town the charred ruins were swept away, and fine new houses, shops and workshops appeared. Described by Daniel Defoe in the 1720s as 'the handsomest and best town in all this part of England', the town was already a noted supplier of footwear to the army, as well as to civilians and the American colonies.

Charles II's gift of timber from the royal forests of Salcey and Whittlebury to the church rebuilding and other matters affected a reconciliation with the town. However, after his death the Catholic James II interfered with this staunchly Protestant and Whiggish town: invoking the charter, during 1688 he ousted a mayor, eight aldermen, the town attorney, 16 ex-bailiffs, the acting bailiffs, 23 common council men and the next mayor-elect. However, James fled the country when William of Orange landed at Torbay later that year.

To the burghers and townsmen of Northampton, the 1688 bloodless revolution ensured the Protestant ascendancy; henceforth they were content and loyal to the Crown, the earlier Civil War episodes forgotten. The town had indeed had

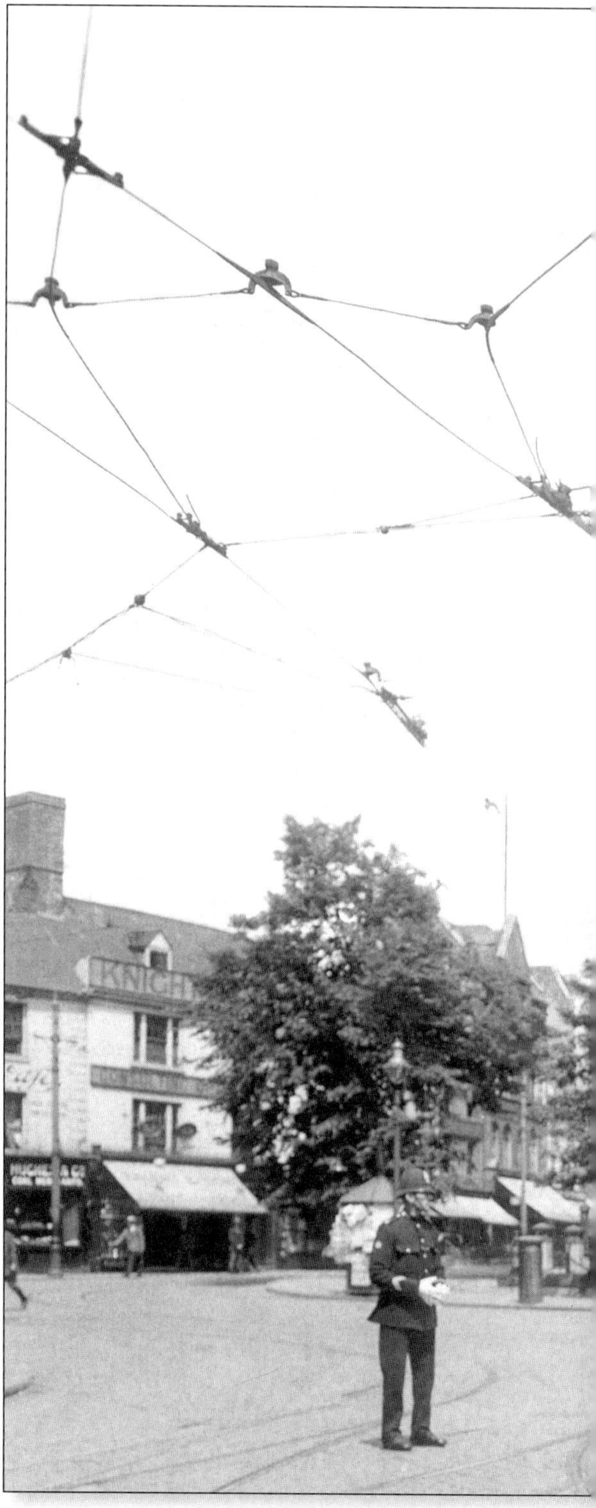

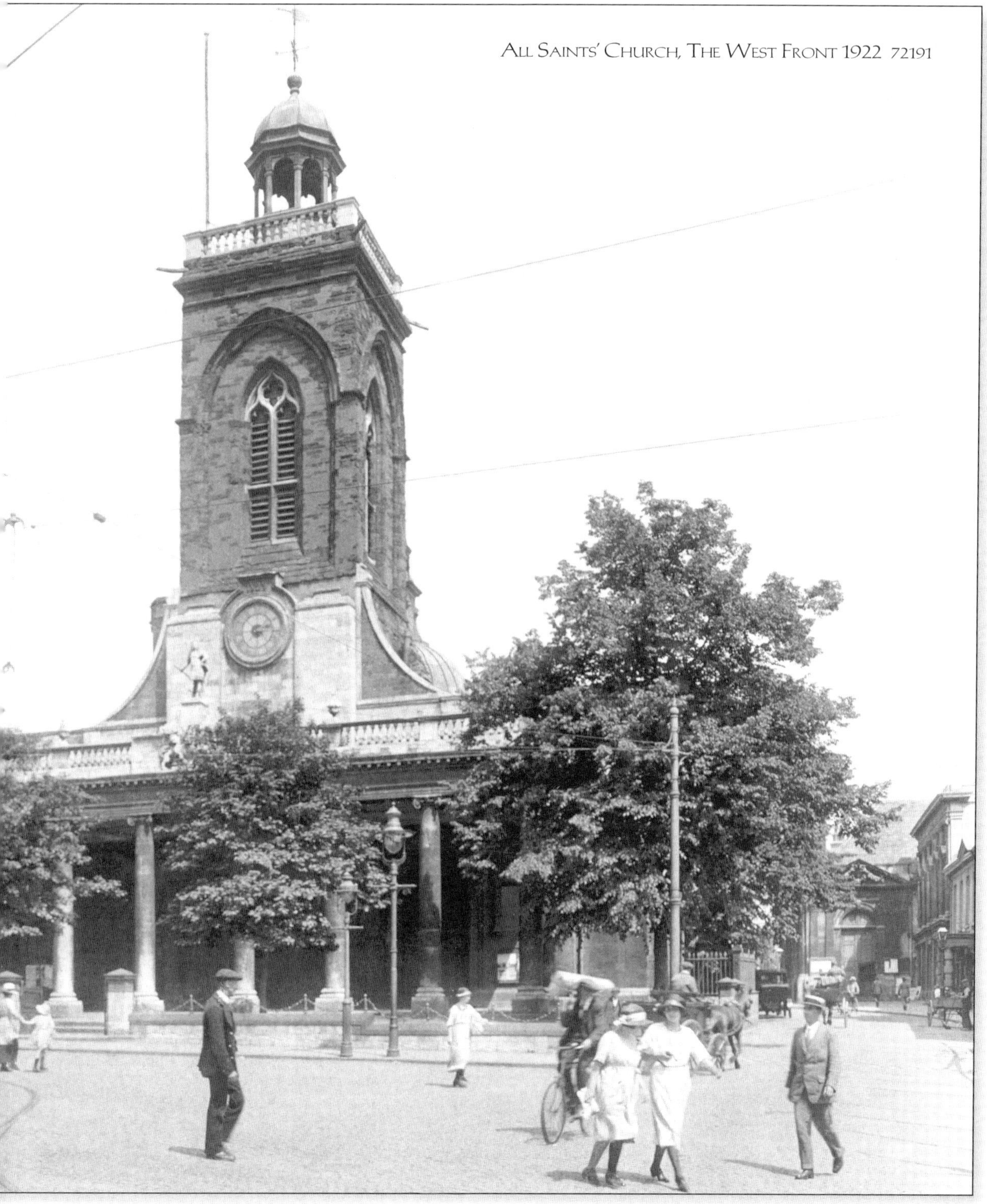

ALL SAINTS' CHURCH, THE WEST FRONT 1922 72191

a long civic history which pre-dates the first recorded charter of 1185, when the burgesses or merchants paid 200 marks to hold their town 'in chief', that is direct from the king. By the time of Domesday Book in 1087 there were 87 royal burgesses holding their tenements direct from the king, as well as 219 holding theirs from other lords, so the town was large and had its own reeve and bailiffs. The reeves had become mayors by 1215 — William Tilly was the first named mayor. The importance of Northampton at this time was underlined by the fact that only London, York and King's Lynn had mayors by this date.

The mayor ruled with a council of twelve, later twenty-four, and the assembly of the town included all freemen, but by an Act of Parliament of 1469 Northampton and Leicester secured a joint de-democratisation of their town governments. The mayor and ex-mayors, later called aldermen, the twenty-four (the ex-bailiffs) and the forty-eight common councillors made up the closed body that ruled the town until 1835. The 'Forty-Eight' common councillors held office for life, and were replaced by co-option, not election. Not surprisingly, it became out of touch with the radicalism of the town and its strong Nonconformist and Whig leanings, and was seen largely as an Anglican and Tory preserve.

Northampton was, of course, the county town for Northamptonshire, and its shire hall was destroyed in the 1675 fire. At this date one of the main functions of a county was the holding of assizes and more local courts, together with some highway matters; the more modern functions of a county council were only acquired later. The Sessions House (72179, pages 32-33, right) was built between 1676 and 1678 on the site of the county gaol, which was rebuilt behind it, but largely demolished in 1930. Opposite is All Saints' Church, and these two key buildings were given a high priority in the resurrection of the fire-consumed town.

Beyond County Hall, towards Bridge Street, is the County Club, 72178, pages 36-37. This was built as the Infirmary in 1744 as the then first hospital outside London; it takes the story on from St John's Hospital, the medieval almshouses in Bridge Street mentioned in Chapter 1. Built as a thirty-bed hospital, the Infirmary was founded by Dr John Stonhouse and the Rev Dr Philip Doddridge, a leading Congregational minister. It soon expanded, and in 1770 reached seventy beds. It outgrew the site, and in 1793 moved to the Billing Road, then outside the town in healthier air.

The new hospital (72183, page 38-39), originally also for

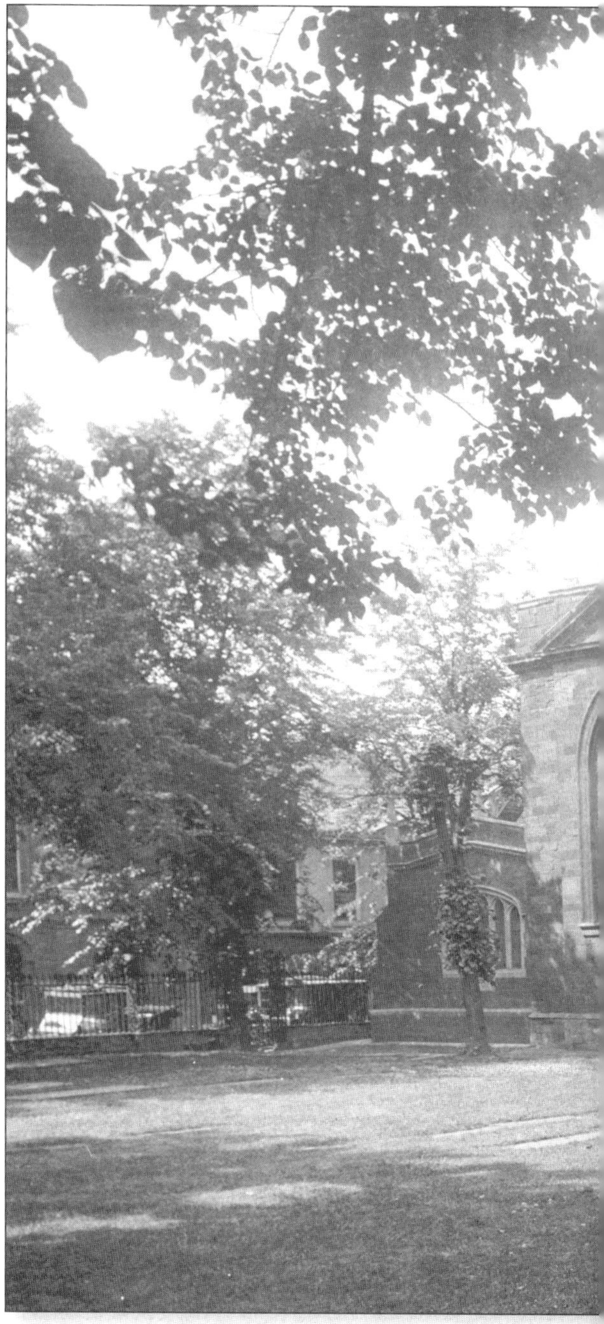

seventy beds, cost £25,000, with several contractors going bankrupt along the way. It was extended in the 1870s and also after that date, but the original front remains, if somewhat swamped by the later additions. In 1804 it began the enlightened practice of free smallpox vaccination of out-patients. Other hospitals included Northampton General Lunatic Asylum, also on the Billing Road, which opened in 1838; it was be replaced in 1876 by the County Asylum at Berry Wood.

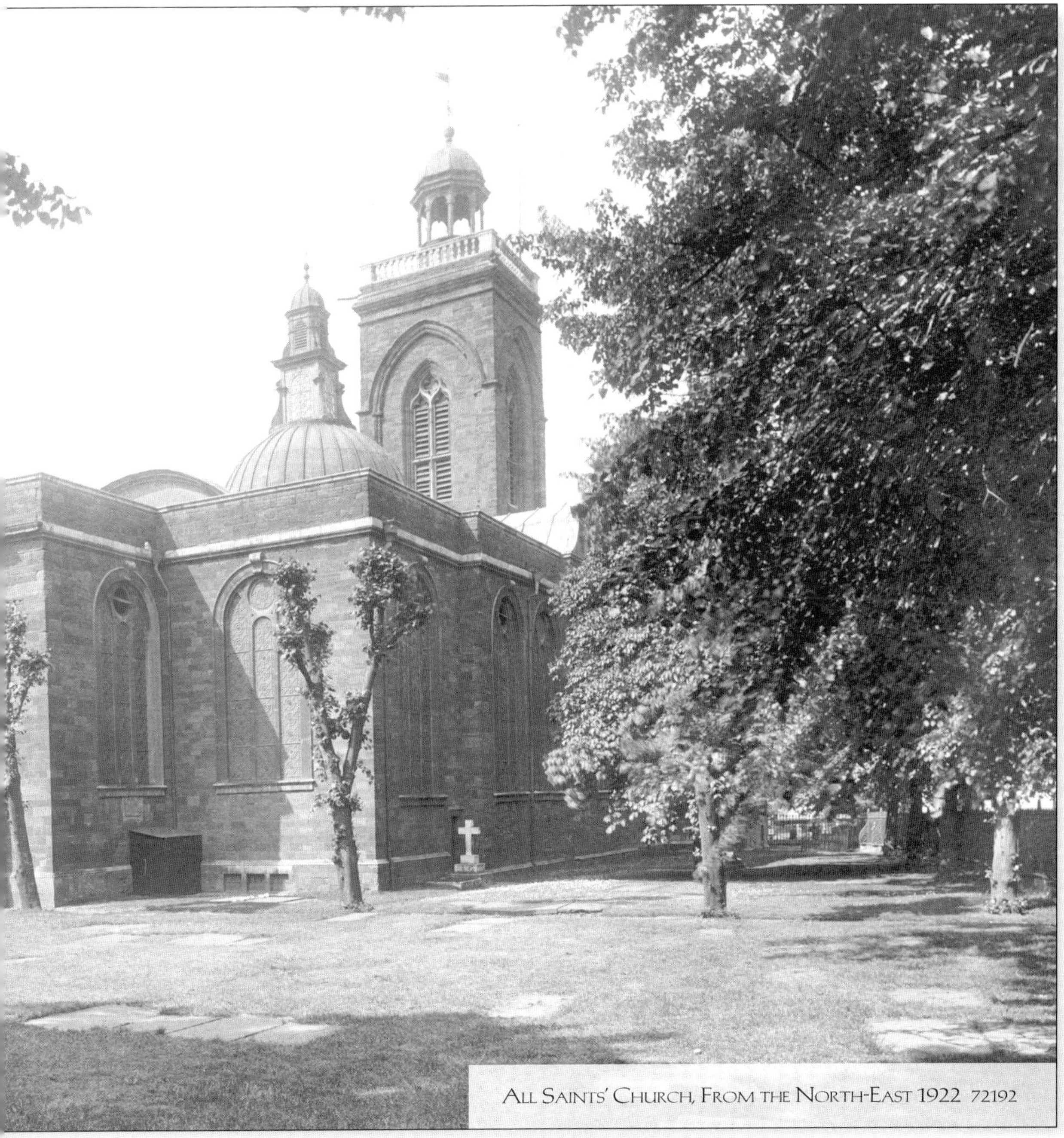

ALL SAINTS' CHURCH, FROM THE NORTH-EAST 1922 72192

"The County Hall stands in George Row; it was erected soon after the great fire of 1675, and extended and re-arranged in 1812. It is an elegant and spacious structure in the Corinthian style; contains courts for the assizes and quarter-sessions, and a commodious suite of rooms for the county business; and is adorned with a splendidly ornate ceiling. The County Council Chamber, erected in 1890 at the back of the County Hall, is a spacious edifice of brick."

BRABNER'S GAZETTEER OF ENGLAND AND WALES 1895

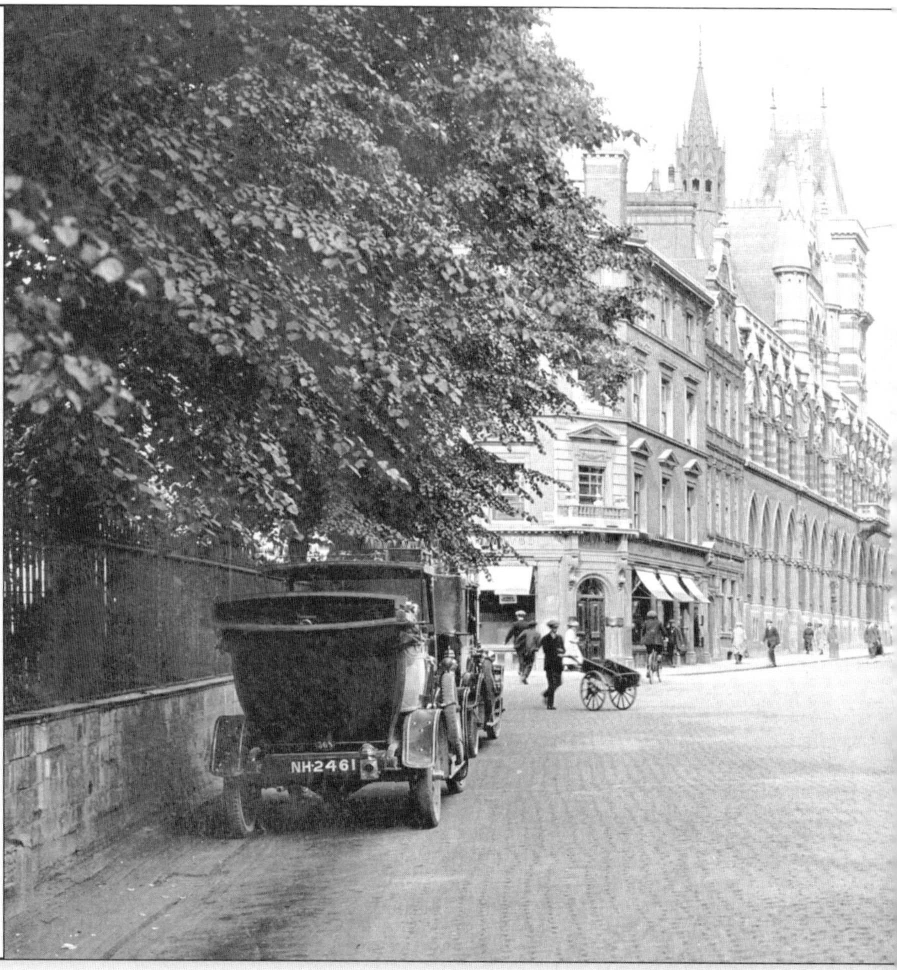

The boot and shoe trade has already been mentioned, and the markets and fairs were also a key element in the town's trading and manufacturing economy. The first reference to a fair is in about 1180: it was held on All Saints' Day in the church and churchyard of All Saints'. In 1235 it moved to a waste area north of the church. This waste became the present spacious Market Place, described in 1712 as 'lookt upon as the finest in Europe; a fair spacious open place'. The fair lasted all of November. The town acquired various weekly markets, with a charter of 1599 confirming Wednesday, Friday and Saturday as market days. Street names in the town give a fair indication of the trades and market centres in the town: for example, Corn Hill, Malt Hill, Mercers Row, Gold Street, Sheep Street and Horse Fair. Market tolls, of course, were a major source of the town's income, and market rights were jealously protected; hence the numerous charters obtained over the centuries.

In the Middle Ages cloth and wool were very important, but

"Northampton received its first charter from Henry II, and it has sent two members to Parliament since the time of Edward I."

BRABNER'S GAZETTEER OF ENGLAND AND WALES 1895

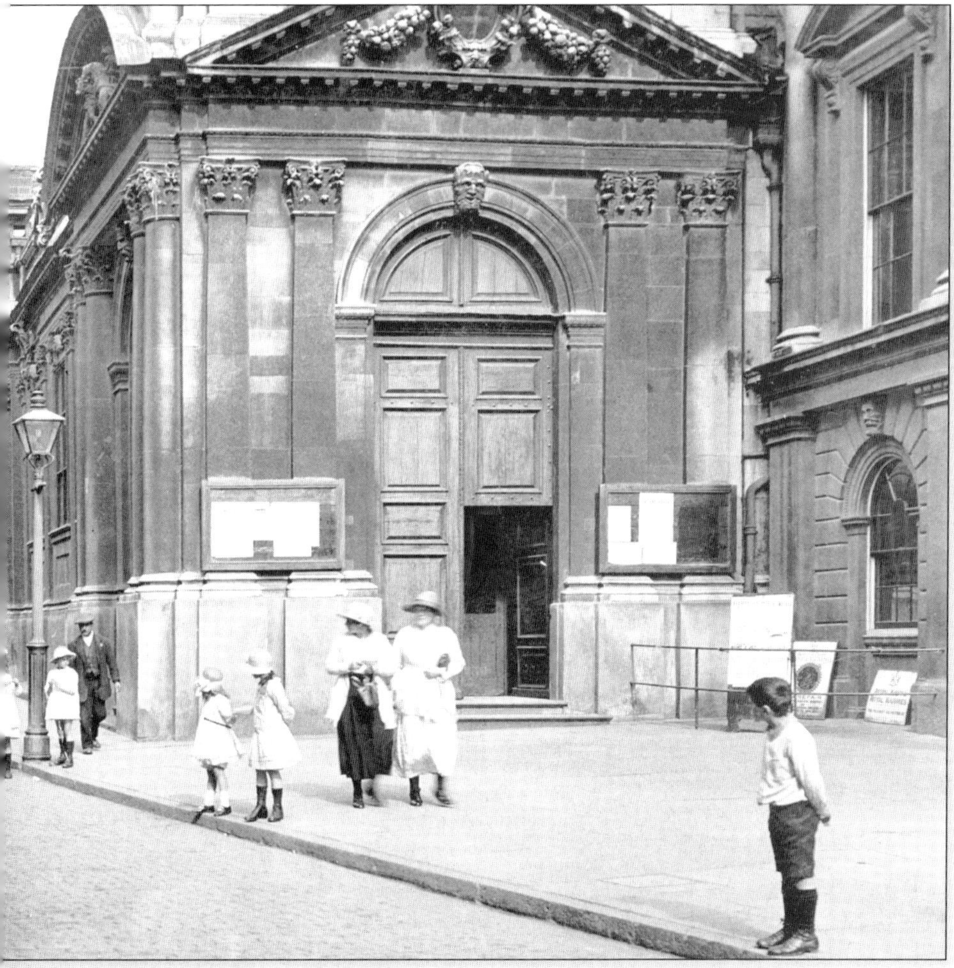

GEORGE ROW 1922
72179

Also rebuilt shortly after the 1675 fire, the County Hall, on the right, also attributed to Henry Bell, has an elaborate façade with semi-circular pediments to the front and a further pediment to the return facing the cameraman. Within are the courthouses of the Sessions House. To the left are the railings and trees of All Saints' churchyard, and beyond is the Victorian Gothic Guildhall.

these industries declined. By 1600 leather-working was pre-eminent, with glove making at this stage as important as shoe making. By the later 17th century, shoes and boots had won, no doubt assisted by the Civil War armies' need for boots and shoes rather than gloves. Until well into the 19th century the shoes were produced in small workshops, often at the bottom of leather workers' gardens, or in their homes; separate trades were established for the various processes, from cutting the leather to sewing and soling.

Until the 19th century, the growth of the town's population was steady and unspectacular, rising from 5,136 in 1746 to 7,020 in 1801. Partly this was because much of the shoe industry was carried on in the surrounding villages. But by 1831 the population had doubled to 15,351, stimulated no doubt by the vast demand for boots for the army during the Napoleonic Wars; a third of the adult males alone were now shoemakers. After the mid-19th century the industry rapidly became mechanised, with factories soon becoming the norm, and by 1901 the town's population had expanded to 90,923. In 1897 Northampton Town Football Club was formed, and soon acquired its nickname of 'The Cobblers'; as over 40% of the town's population was by now employed in the boot and shoe trade, this was an eminently reasonable nickname.

In 1835 the old oligarchic Tory corporation was reformed, and a democratically-elected council replaced it — or one at least as democratic as such things were before universal suffrage.

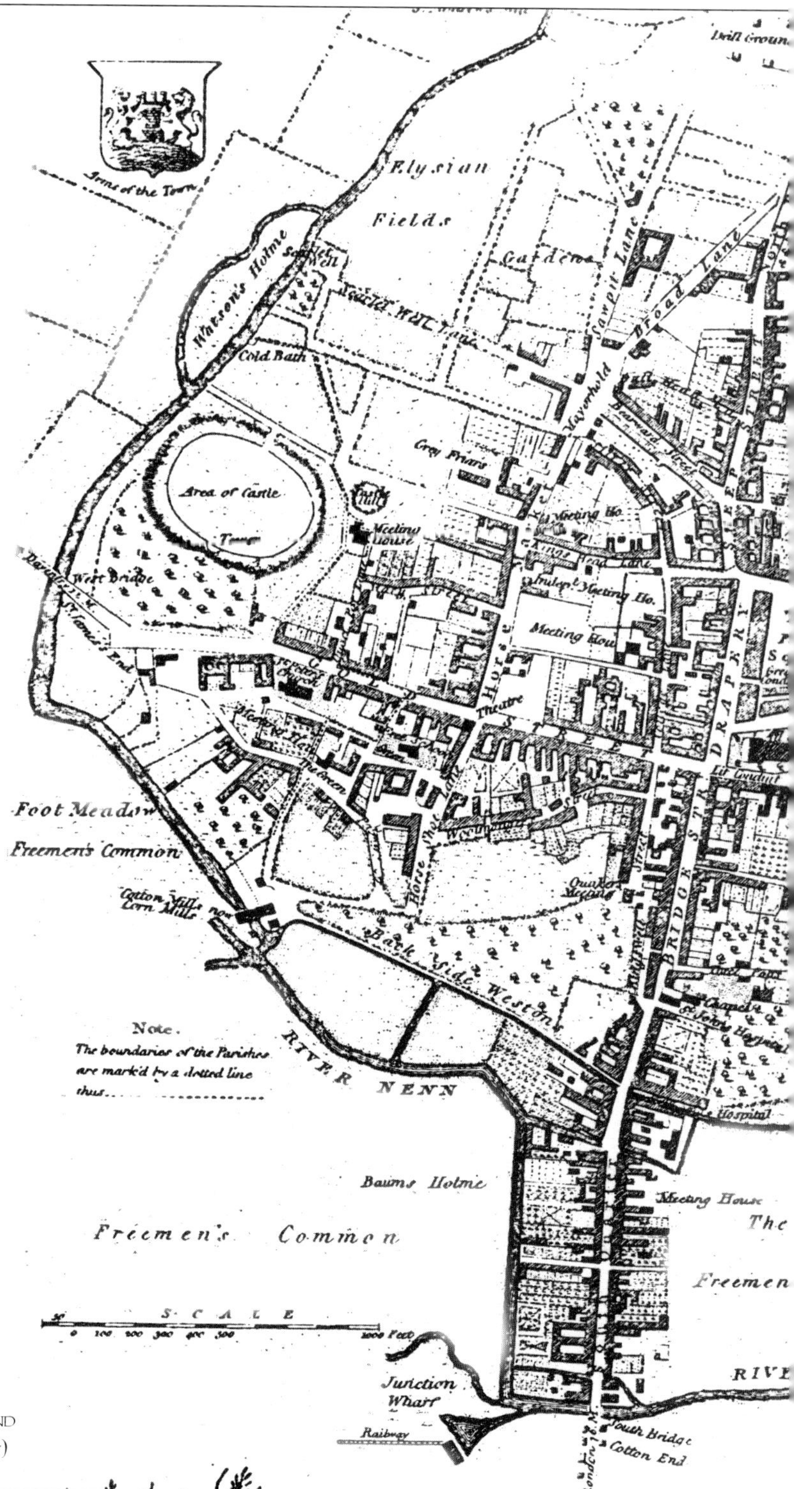

Plan of Northampton in 1810, from John Britton 'The Beauties of England and Wales'. Reproduced by kind permission of Northampton Central Library)

TO VICTORIAN MUNICIPAL PRIDE

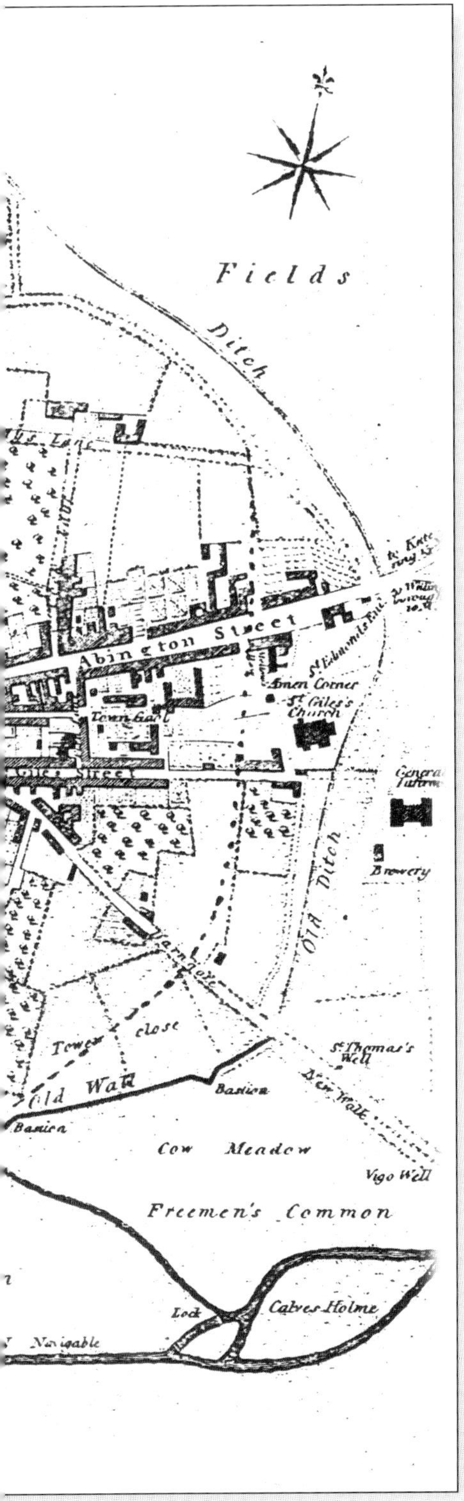

Town government now alternated between Liberals and Conservatives, with the town achieving independence from Northamptonshire in 1888 when it became a county borough.

By the 1860s, the corporation was feeling cramped in the 15th-century Guildhall; as the new Conservative mayor, Christopher Markham, pointed out, it would long ago have been replaced but for the 'great control the ratepayers really exercised over the gentlemen sent there to take care of their pockets'. Following an architectural competition, which was won by Edward Godwin of Bristol, the foundation stone was laid in 1861, and the building formally opened in 1864. Besides council chambers and offices there was a library, which was intended to raise the standards of the local workers' education. The views in this book show the Guildhall after it was extended in the same style by Matthew Holding in 1889-1892, virtually doubling it in width.

The common fields of Northampton were enclosed in the 1780s; the commons were retained and vested in the corporation. These included the Race Course, now Race Course Recreation Ground, and Cow Meadow, now Beckett's Park open space, and other meadows along the River Nene valley (see pages 42). The west part of Cow Meadow was built over as the old cattle market in the 1870s, which has now been replaced.

Cow Meadow had a dual purpose as far back as 1703, when pleasure walks were laid out and avenues of trees planted. A chalybeate spring here raised hopes of Northampton aping Bath or Buxton as a spa town, and in 1784 a new walk was laid out from Beckett's Well to this spring, Vigo Well — fences were erected to separate the quality from the cows. Renamed rather more grandly Beckett's Park, it is one of the town's best parks, and makes good use of the River Nene along its south side.

The River Nene was an important trade artery in the earlier Middle Ages, but the town declined as those nearer the sea prospered. It was not until the canal age that Northampton again had good water routes for its trade. The Grand Junction Canal reached the town in 1815 as a branch from Gayton Junction. In a mere five miles it has no less than 17 locks, and merges with the Nene Navigation.

The London to Birmingham Railway passed four miles west of the town in the 1830s, a fact seen by some, including Brabner's 'Gazetteer', as 'a great mistake'; but in truth Northampton was off the route, which had itself been shifted westward by fox-hunting landowners. The railway did arrive in 1845 as a line from Blisworth Junction to Peterborough. Other lines followed, and the final indignity for the site of Northampton Castle was to have a goods shed and goods yard built over the site of the bailey and keep in 1876, expanding the area lost to Castle Station in 1859.

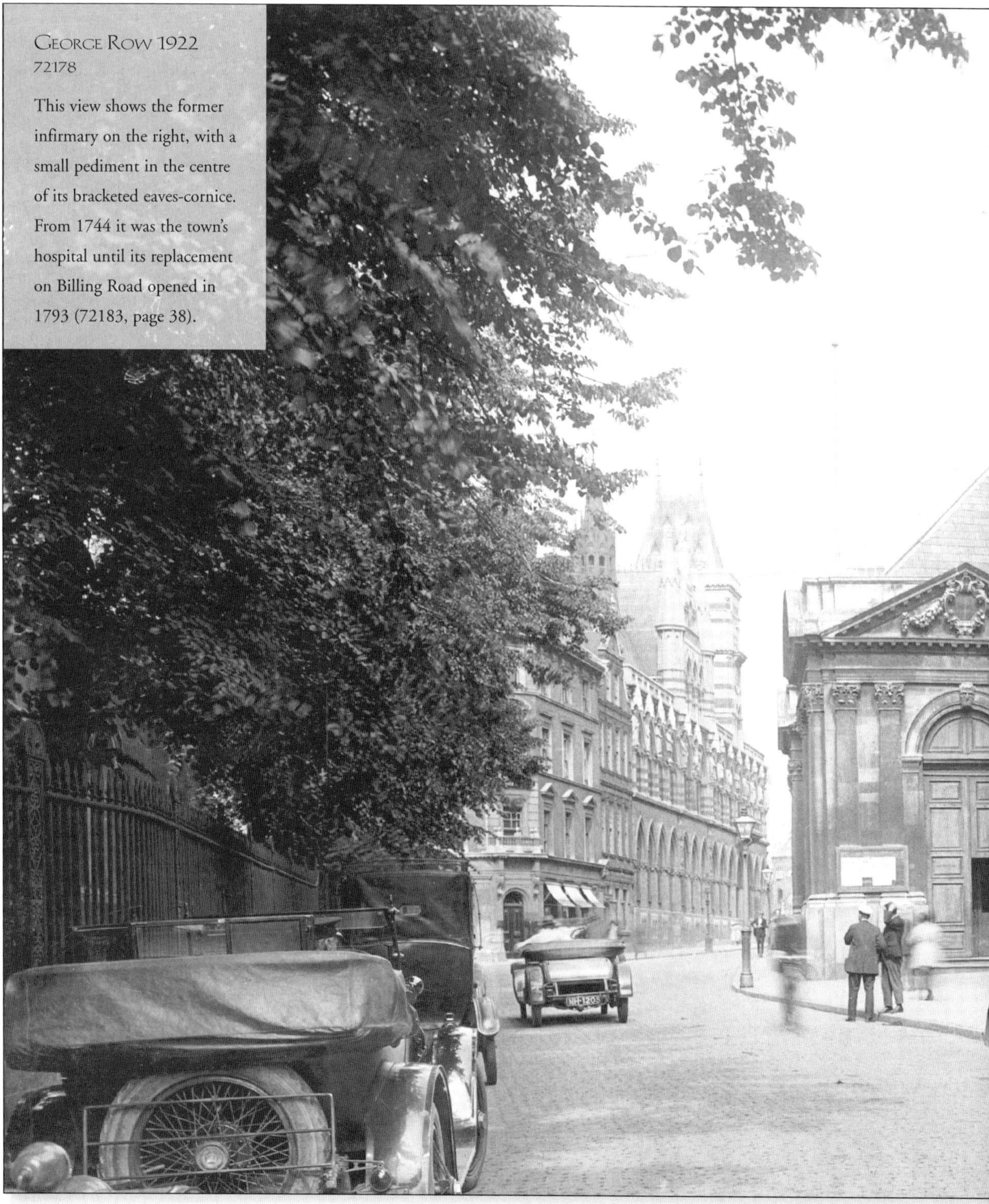

GEORGE ROW 1922
72178

This view shows the former infirmary on the right, with a small pediment in the centre of its bracketed eaves-cornice. From 1744 it was the town's hospital until its replacement on Billing Road opened in 1793 (72183, page 38).

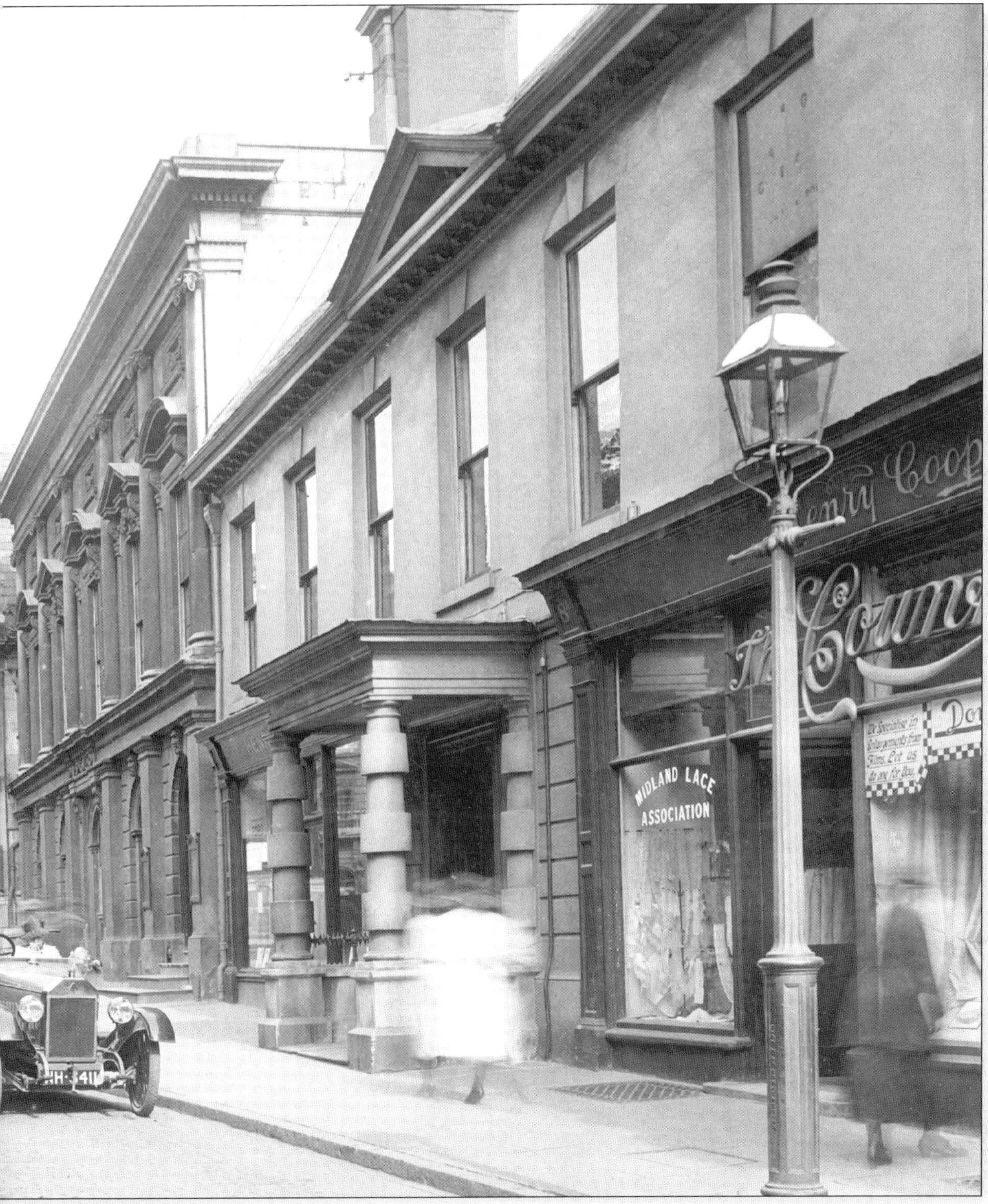
MIDLAND LACE
ASSOCIATION

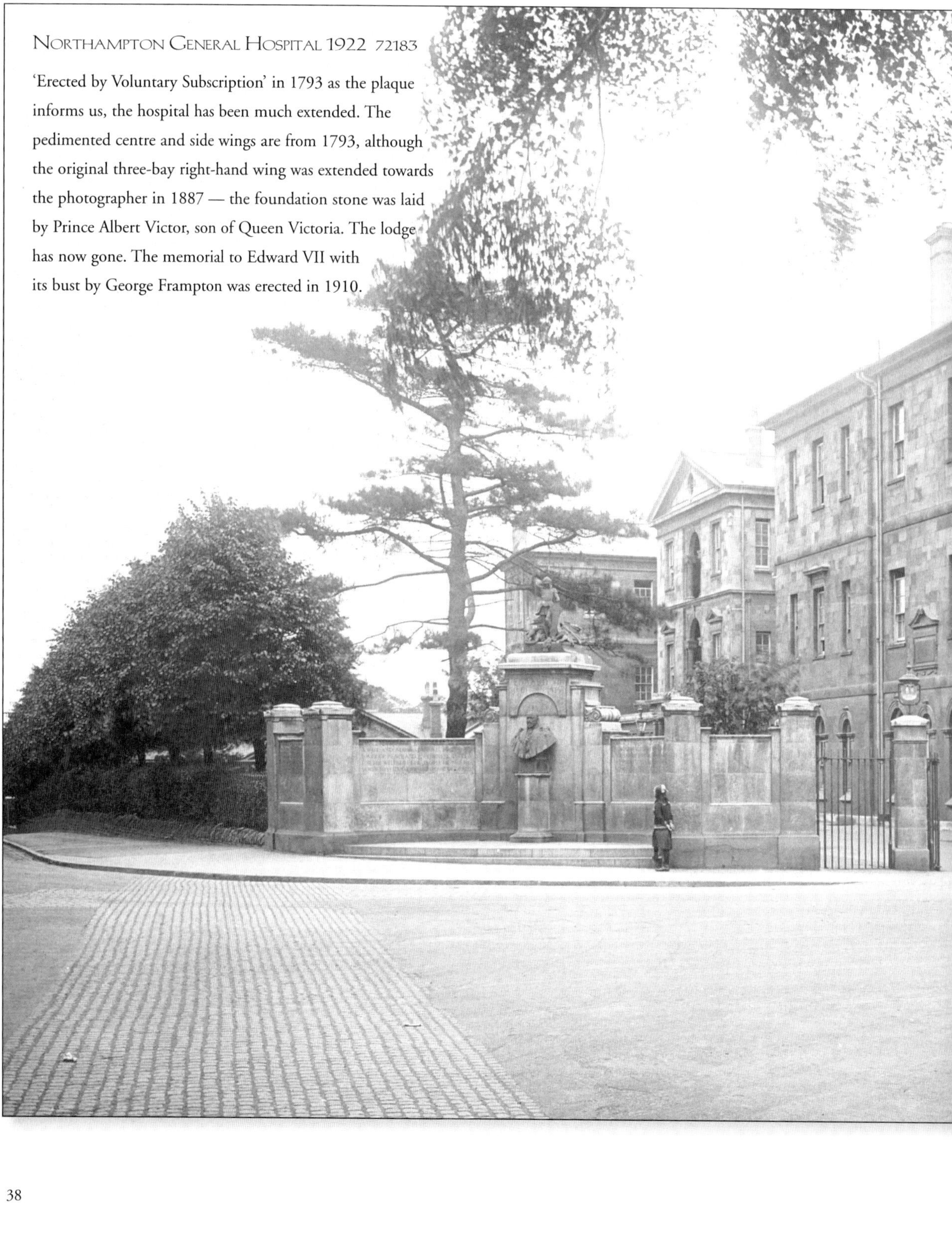

NORTHAMPTON GENERAL HOSPITAL 1922 72183

'Erected by Voluntary Subscription' in 1793 as the plaque informs us, the hospital has been much extended. The pedimented centre and side wings are from 1793, although the original three-bay right-hand wing was extended towards the photographer in 1887 — the foundation stone was laid by Prince Albert Victor, son of Queen Victoria. The lodge has now gone. The memorial to Edward VII with its bust by George Frampton was erected in 1910.

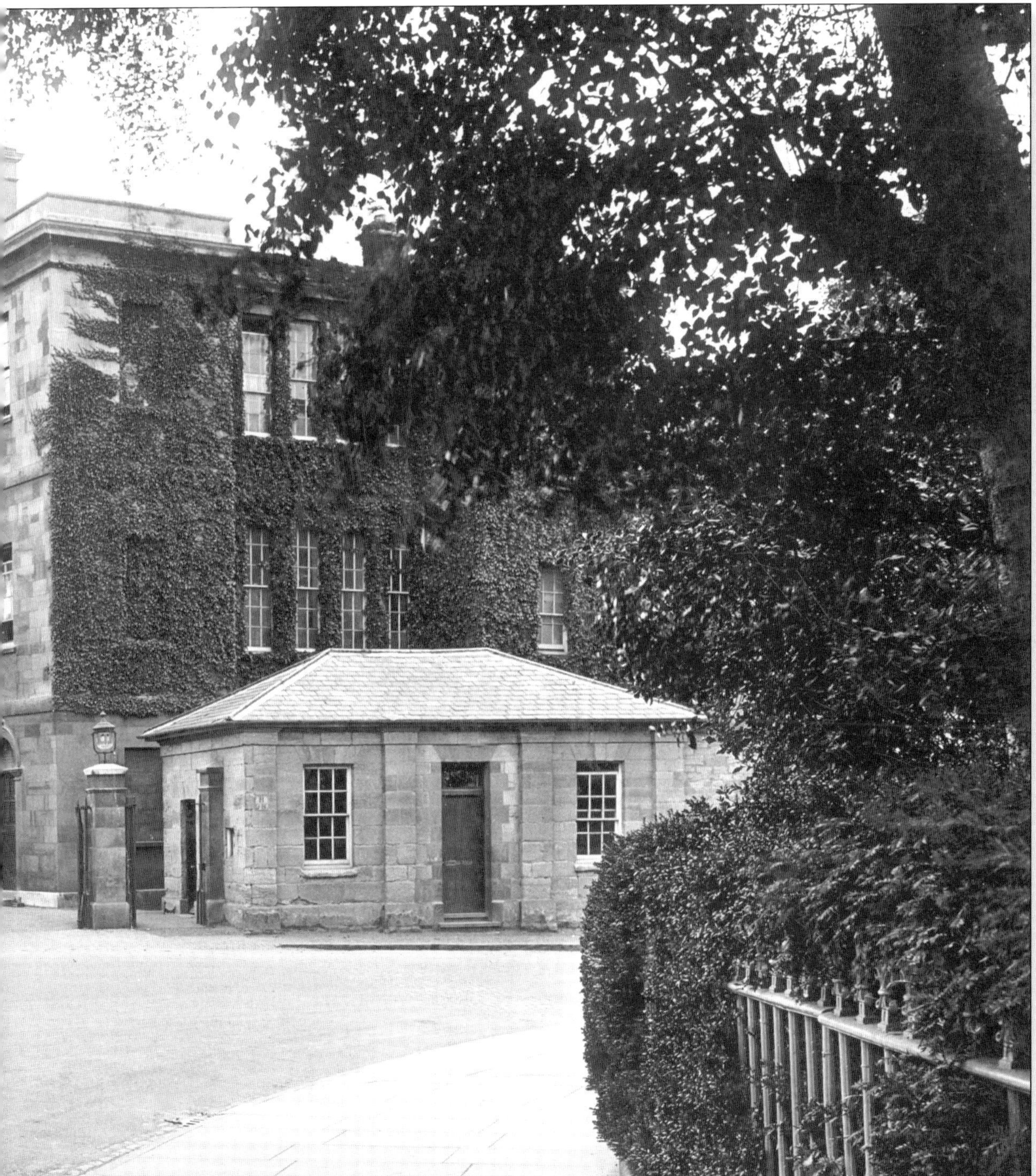

"The Borough – It is now governed by a mayor, 6 aldermen, and 18 councillors, with the usual assistant officers under the title of the Mayor, Bailiffs, and Burgesses of Northampton. By the Local Government Act of 1888 the town was declared a 'county borough' for certain purposes."

BRABNER'S GAZETTEER OF ENGLAND AND WALES 1895

The Guildhall 1922 72181

From the 15th century until the 1860s, the Town Hall, or Guildhall, stood at the south-west corner of Abington Street, looking into the Market Place. By the 1860s it had long been inadequate, and in a spurt of civic pride it was replaced, following an architecturalcompetition, in St Giles Square. This view shows the Guildhall after it was extended in 1889-92: the seven bays to the right are Ernest Godwin's original 1861-64 building — the clock-tower was central then. Matthew Holding added the six bays at the left, and improved the building's scale and grandeur immensely. The result was a Gothic town hall to match many a medieval one in Flanders and northern France, according to locals.

"In former times many trade guilds existed among the burgesses and the craftsmen, one of the most important being that of the shoemakers, whose trade had become the principal in Northampton before the reign of Edward VI."

"Fuller wrote concerning the town 'that it may be said to stand chiefly on other men's legs'; and an old saying asserts that 'you know when you are within a mile of Northampton by the smell of the leather and the noise of the lapstones'."

BRABNER'S GAZETTEER OF ENGLAND AND WALES 1895

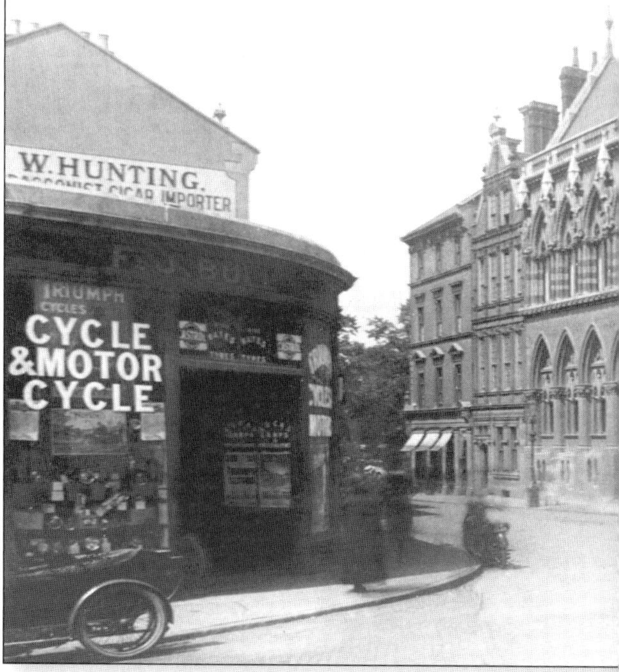

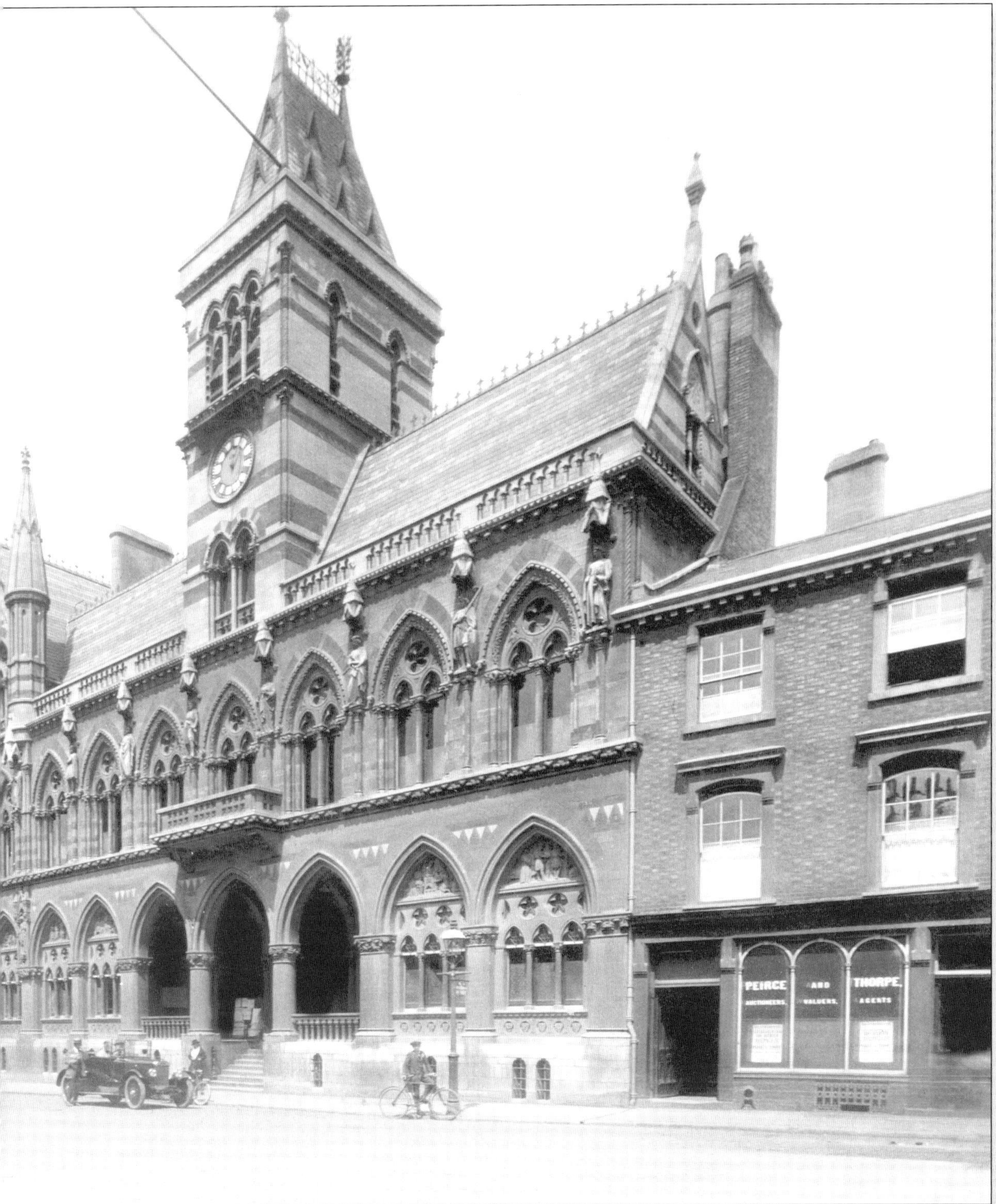
PEIRCE AND THORPE,
AUCTIONEERS, VALUERS, AGENTS

Below: BECKETT'S PARK c1955 N40028

Originally common grazing meadows for the town, Cow Meadow began to be formalised after 1703 when the first avenues and walks were laid out across the pasture. It was hoped that Vigo Well, at its east end, would turn Northampton into a spa town. As it was, the meadows became parkland and were renamed the more toney Beckett's Park in 1935. Bedford Road Promenade led downhill towards the former well; Beckett's Well is just out of view to the left. The other view (72184) was taken looking across the park to the River Nene and its footbridge.

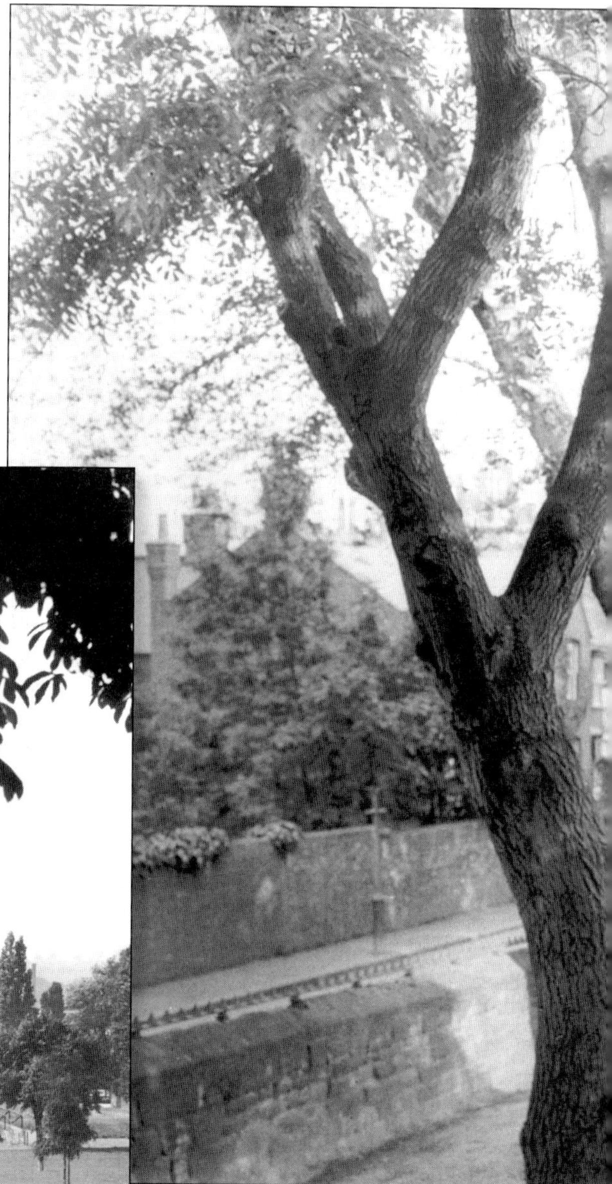

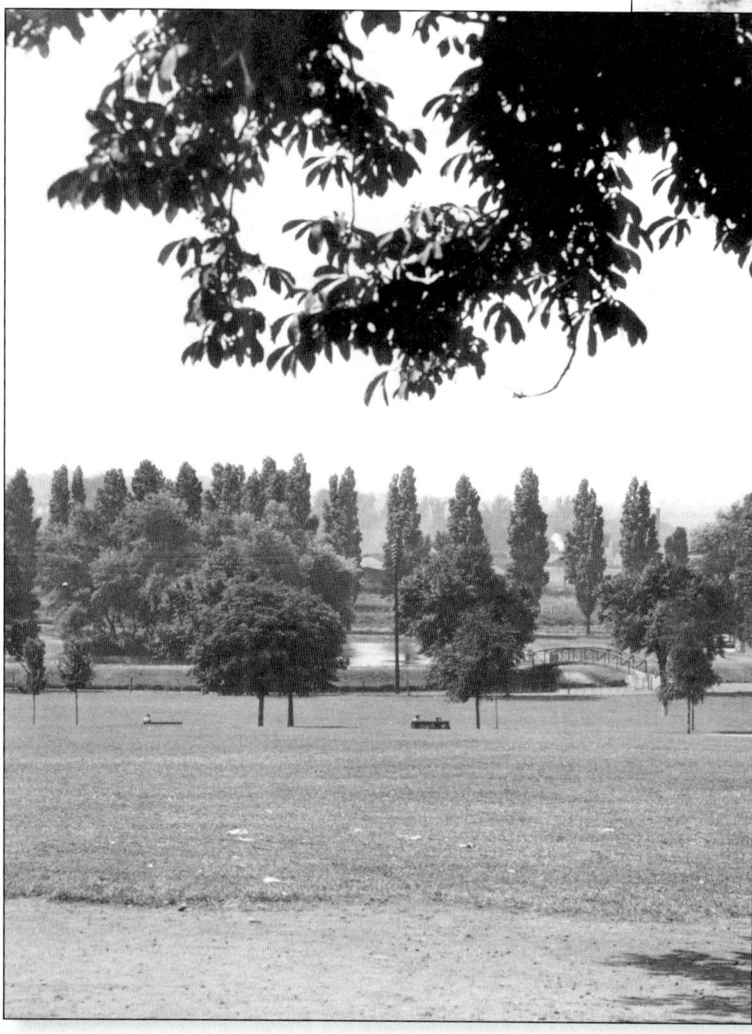

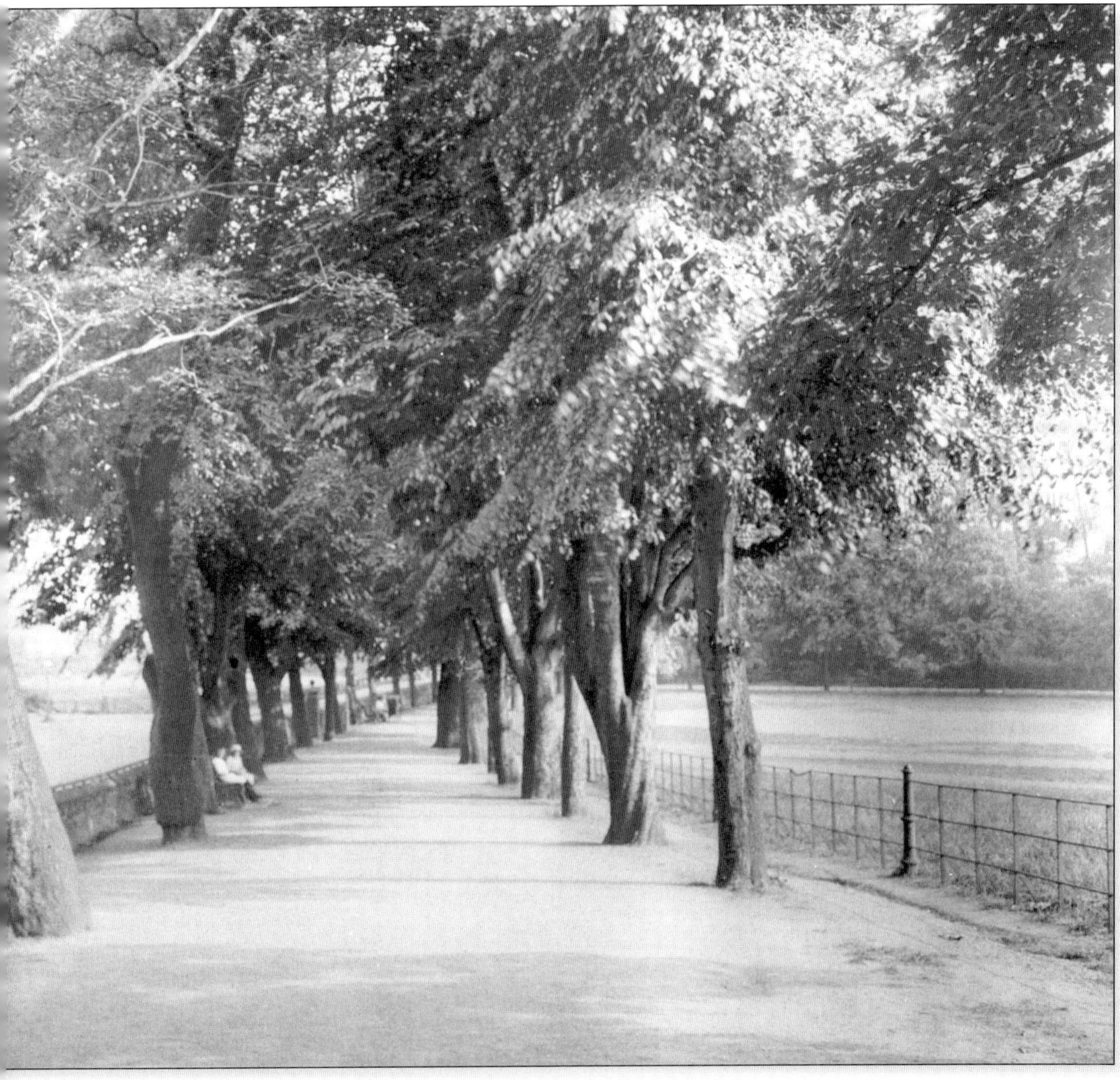

BEDFORD ROAD PROMENADE, BECKETT'S PARK 1922 72184

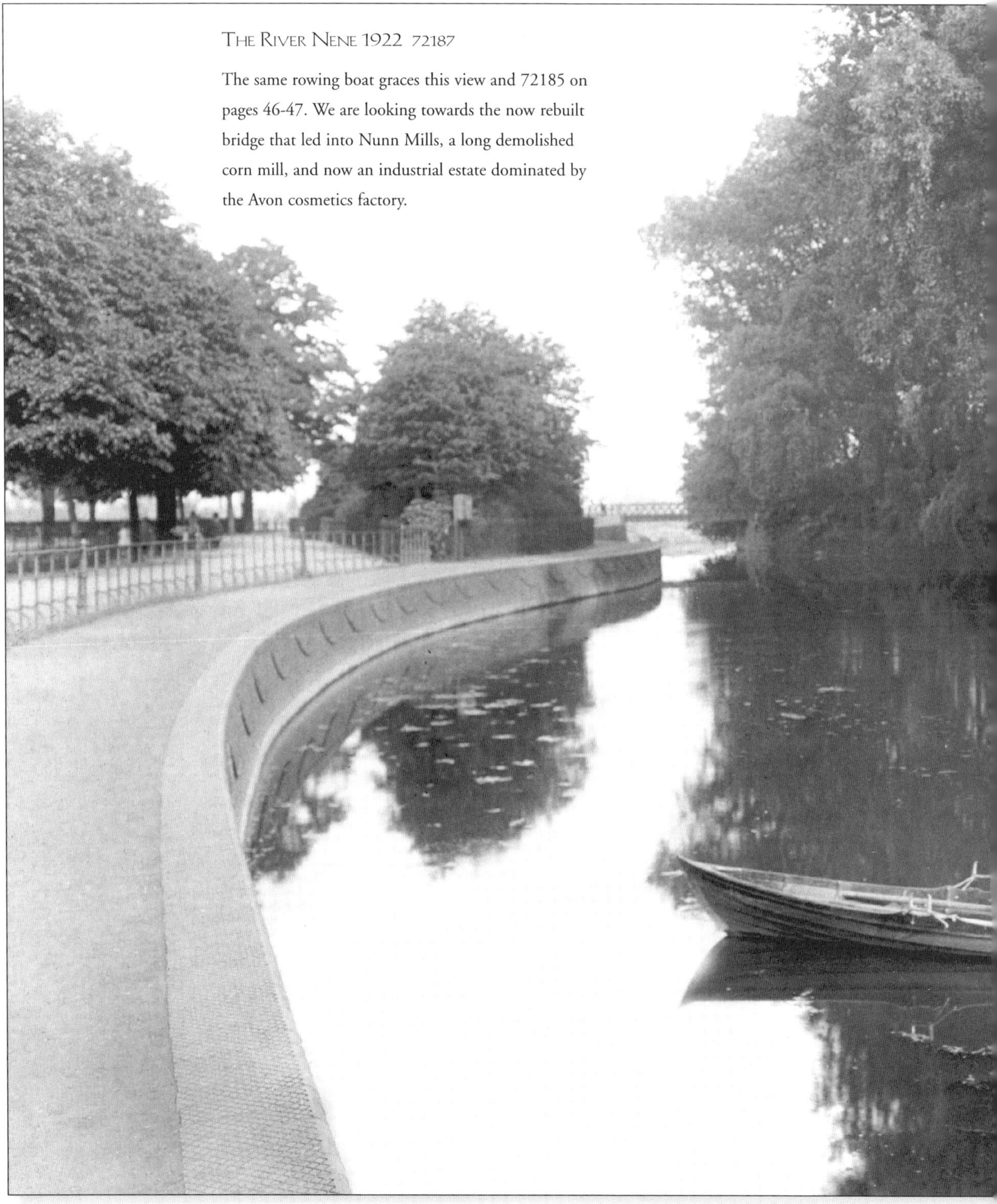

THE RIVER NENE 1922 72187

The same rowing boat graces this view and 72185 on pages 46-47. We are looking towards the now rebuilt bridge that led into Nunn Mills, a long demolished corn mill, and now an industrial estate dominated by the Avon cosmetics factory.

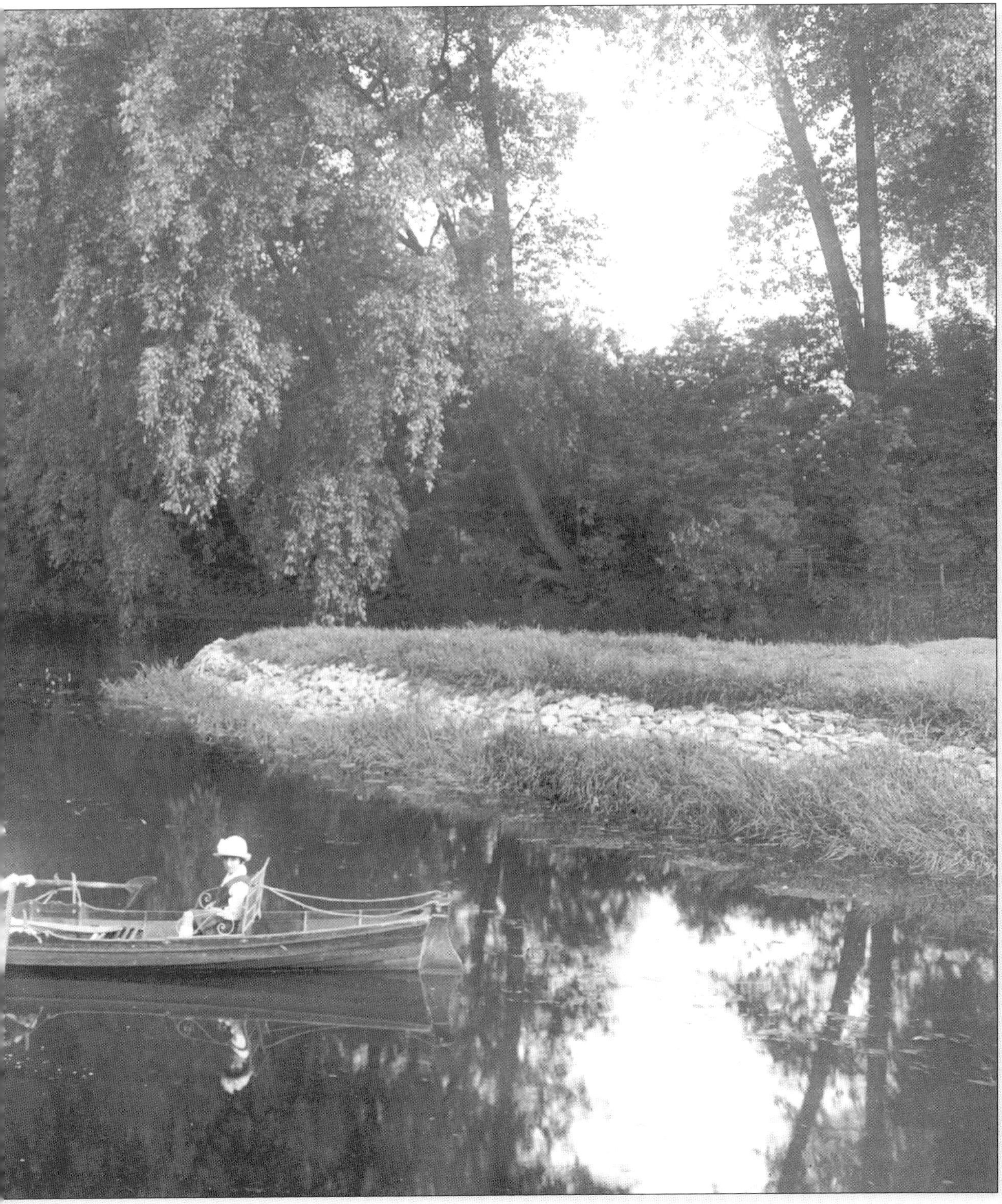

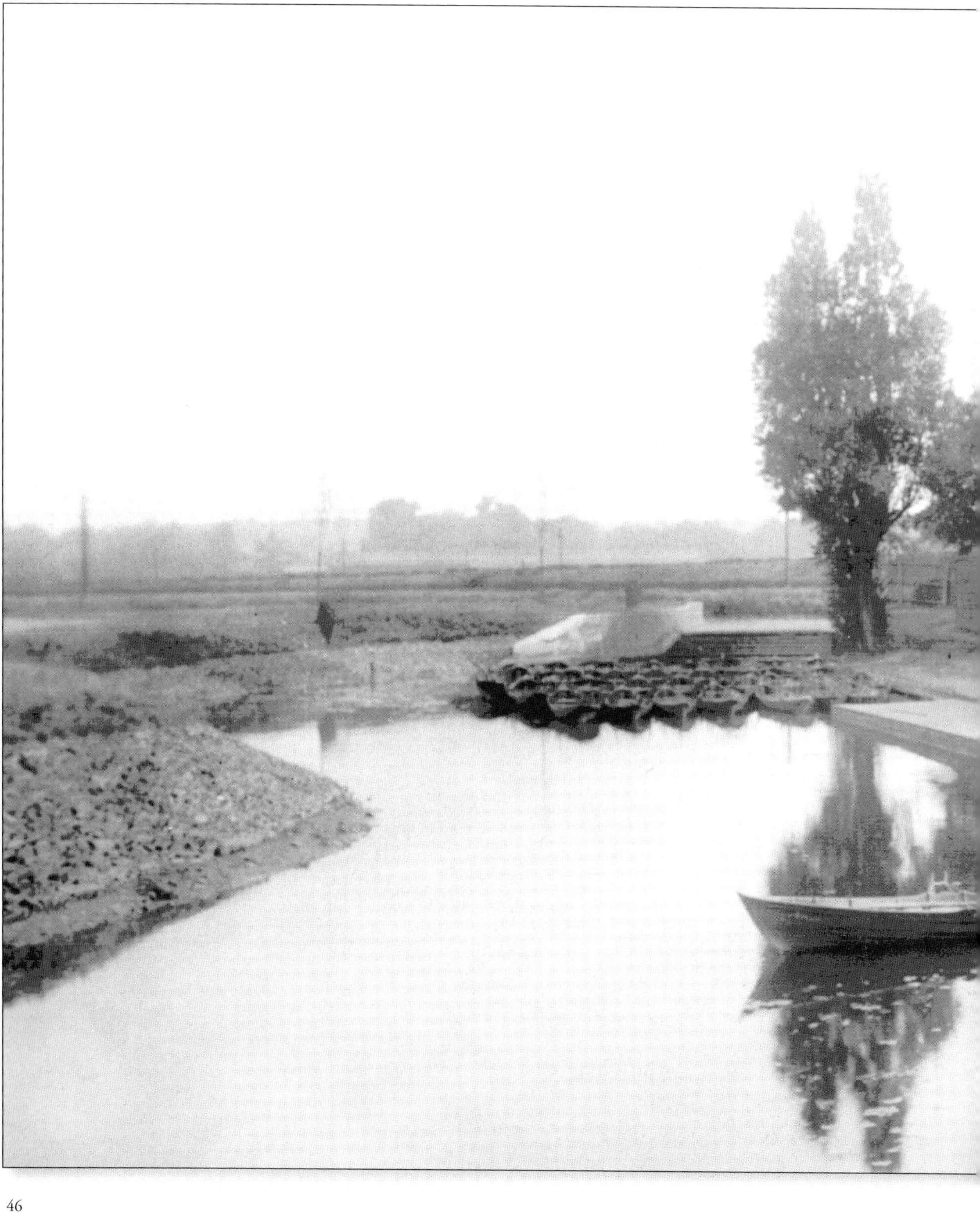

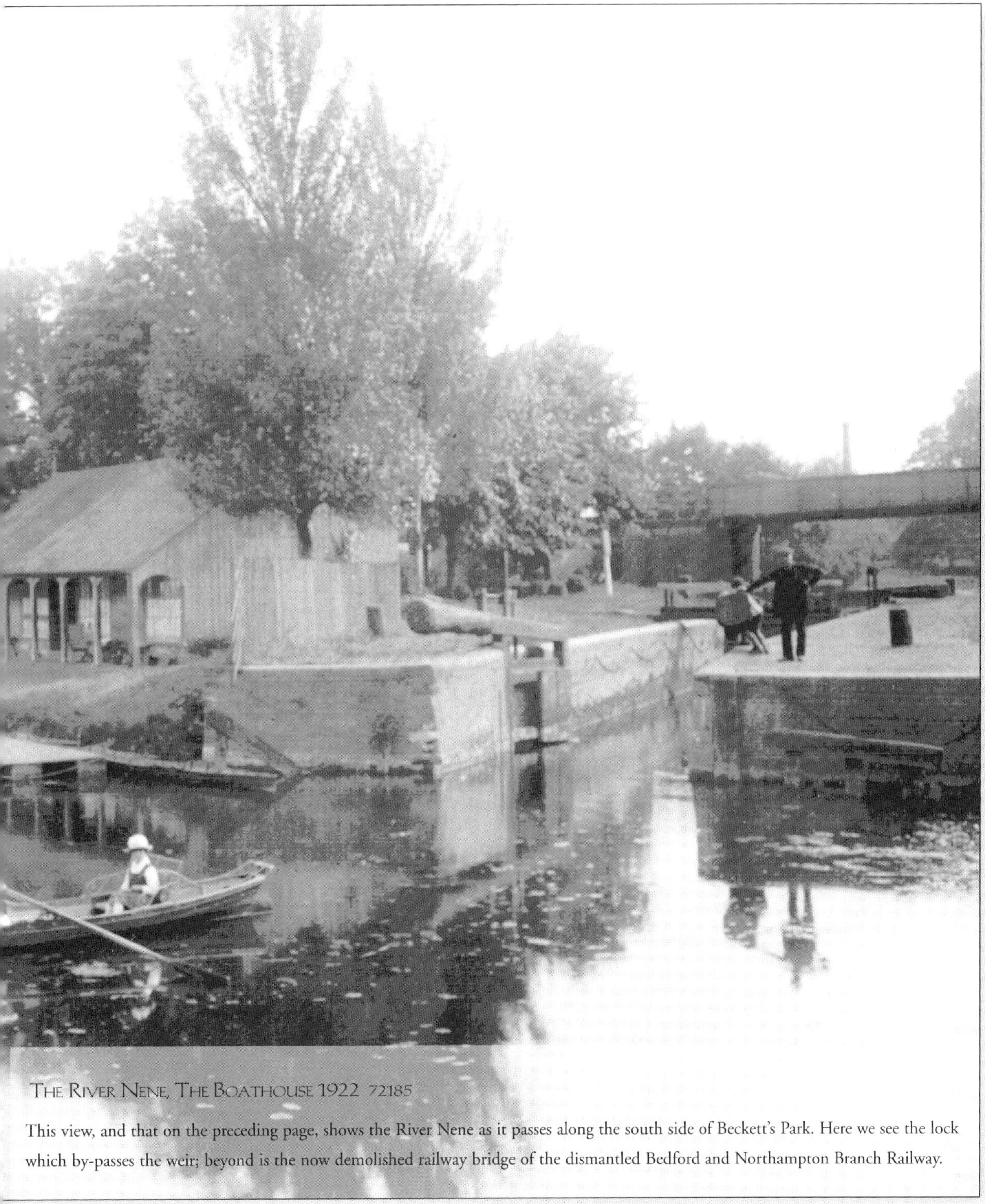

THE RIVER NENE, THE BOATHOUSE 1922 72185

This view, and that on the preceding page, shows the River Nene as it passes along the south side of Beckett's Park. Here we see the lock which by-passes the weir; beyond is the now demolished railway bridge of the dismantled Bedford and Northampton Branch Railway.

Ordnance Survey Map

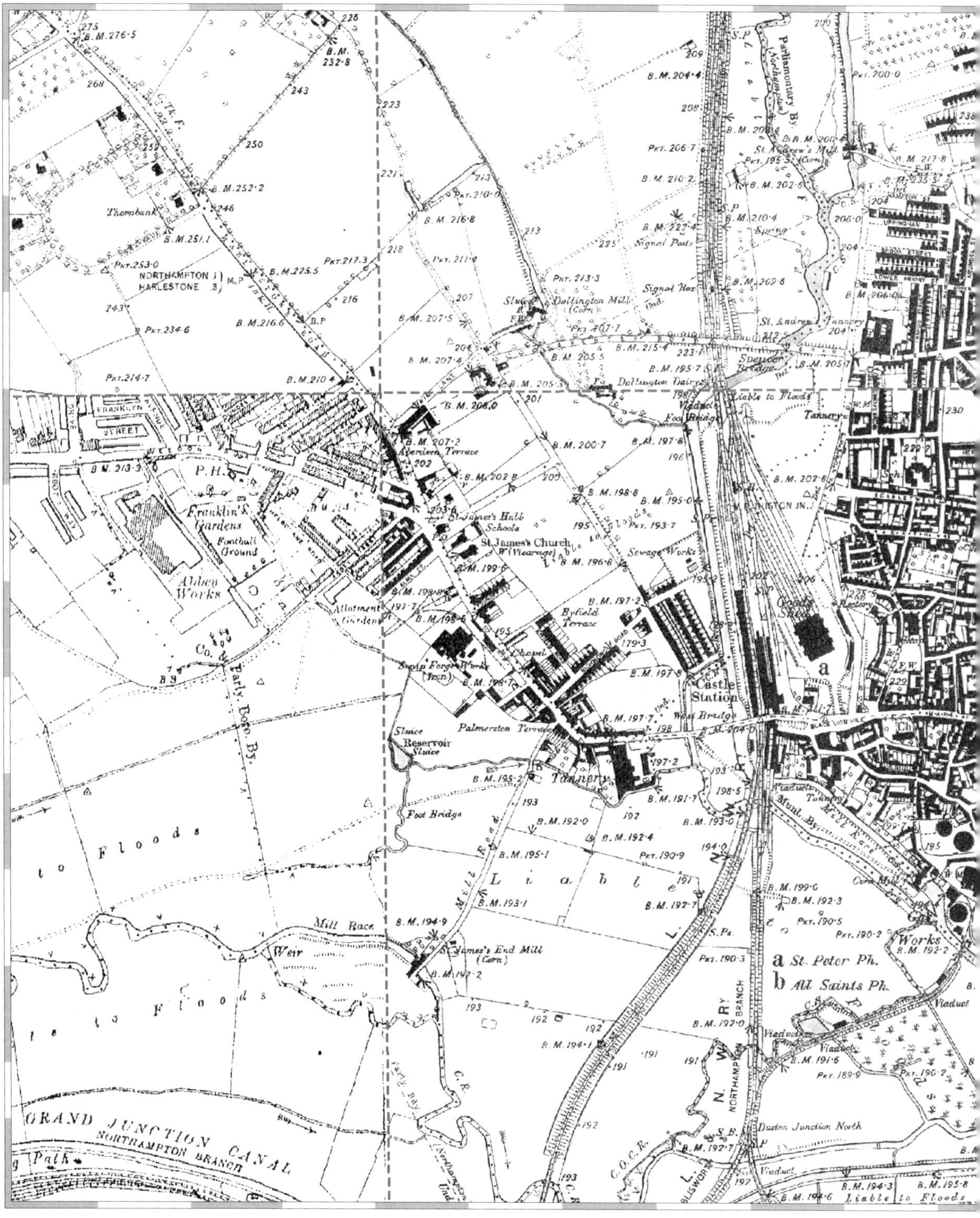

Ordnance Survey Map

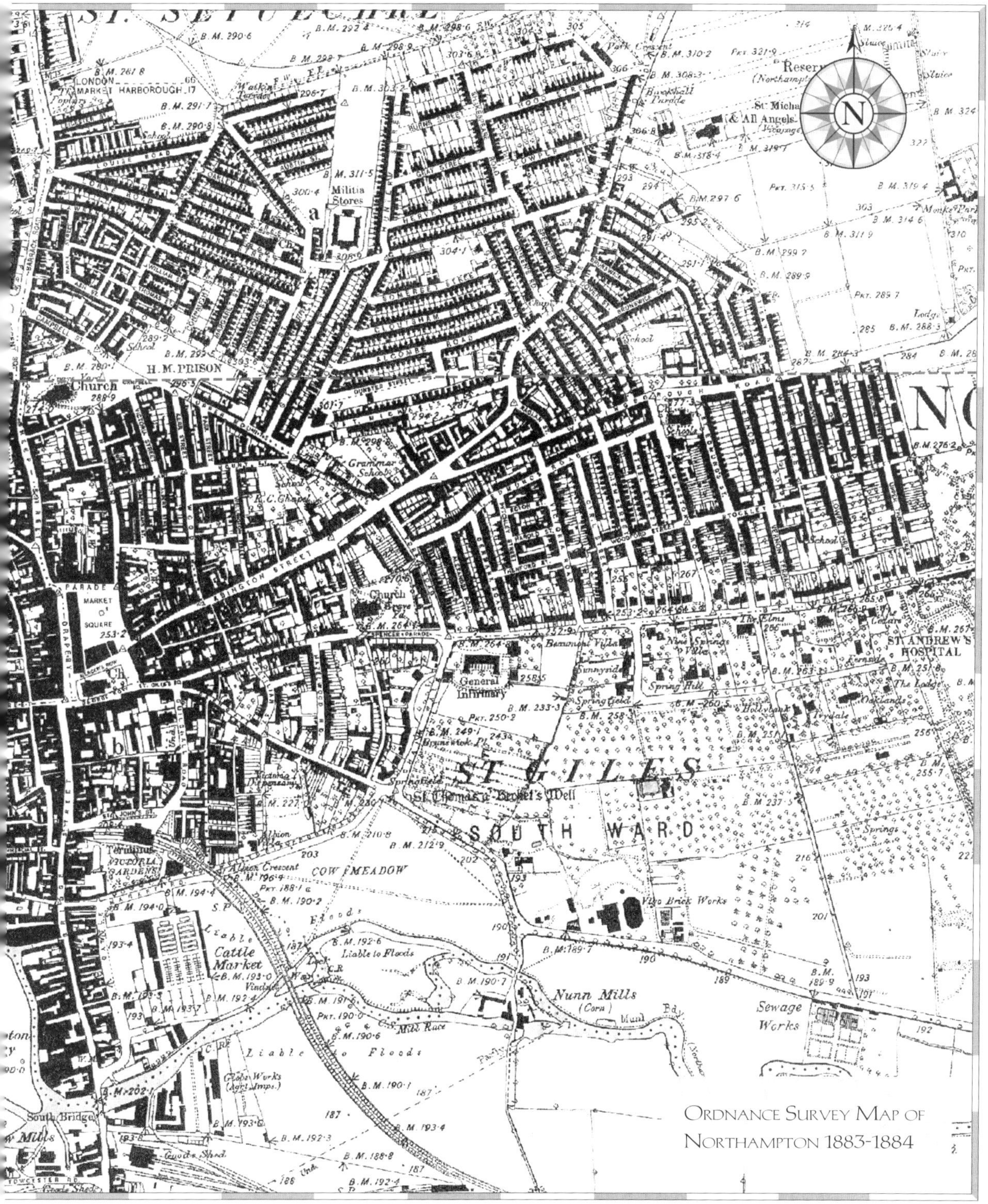

Ordnance Survey Map of
Northampton 1883-1884

THE 1920s:

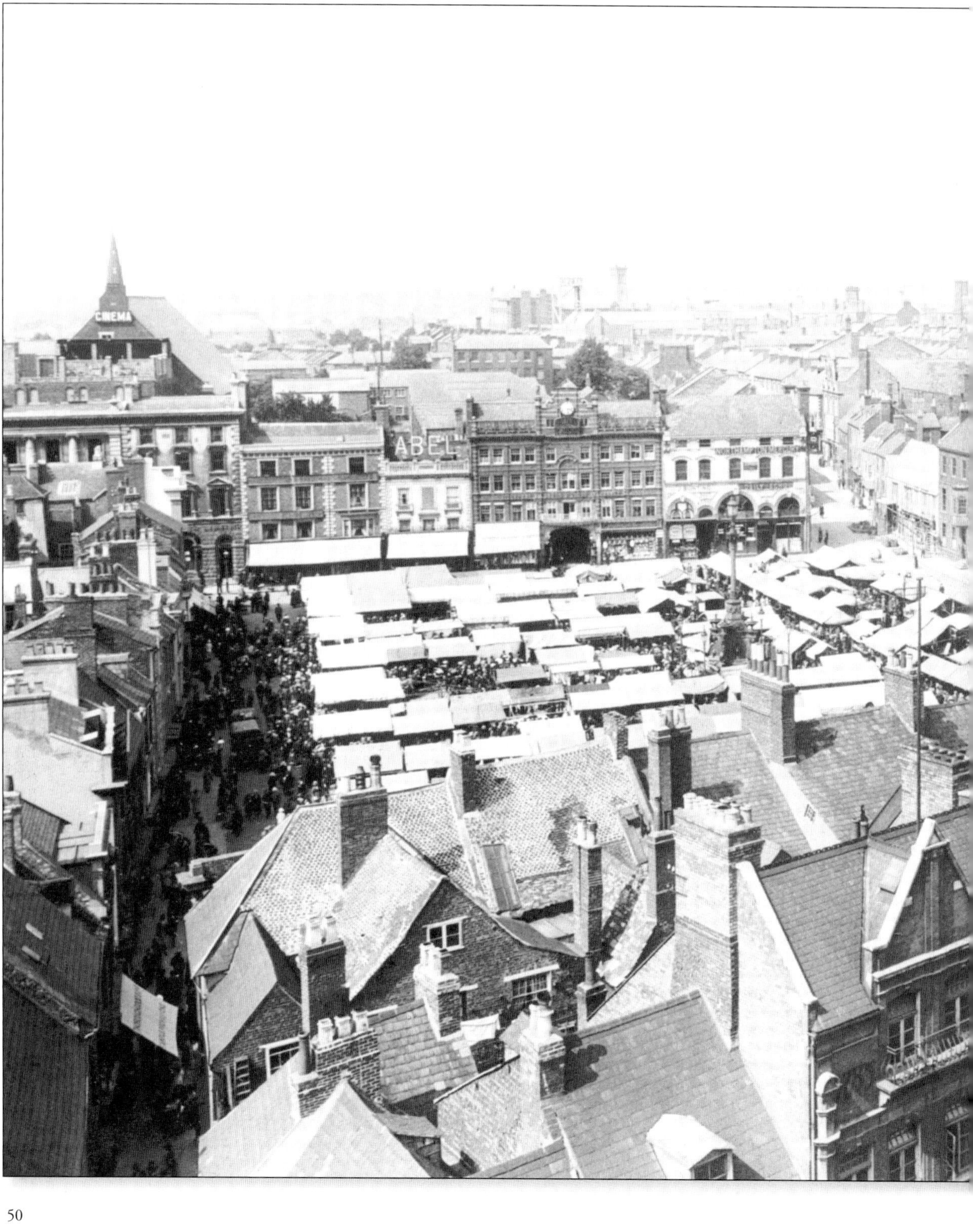

THE STREETS OF NORTHAMPTON

THE MARKET PLACE, FROM THE TOWER OF ALL SAINTS' CHURCH 1922 *72166*

This view and the one on pages 52-52 were taken looking out over the Market Place. Frith's photographer was looking north-east, with the entrance to Abington Street on the right with its curving tramlines. In 72167 (next page) he was looking north, with the Drapery on the left. In both in the background is a tall building with 'Cinema' picked out in large letters. This is the former Corn Exchange, which opened in 1851 and later became a theatre and music hall. In 1920 it became a cinema, the Exchange, which closed in 1974. It is now a Chicago Rock Café.

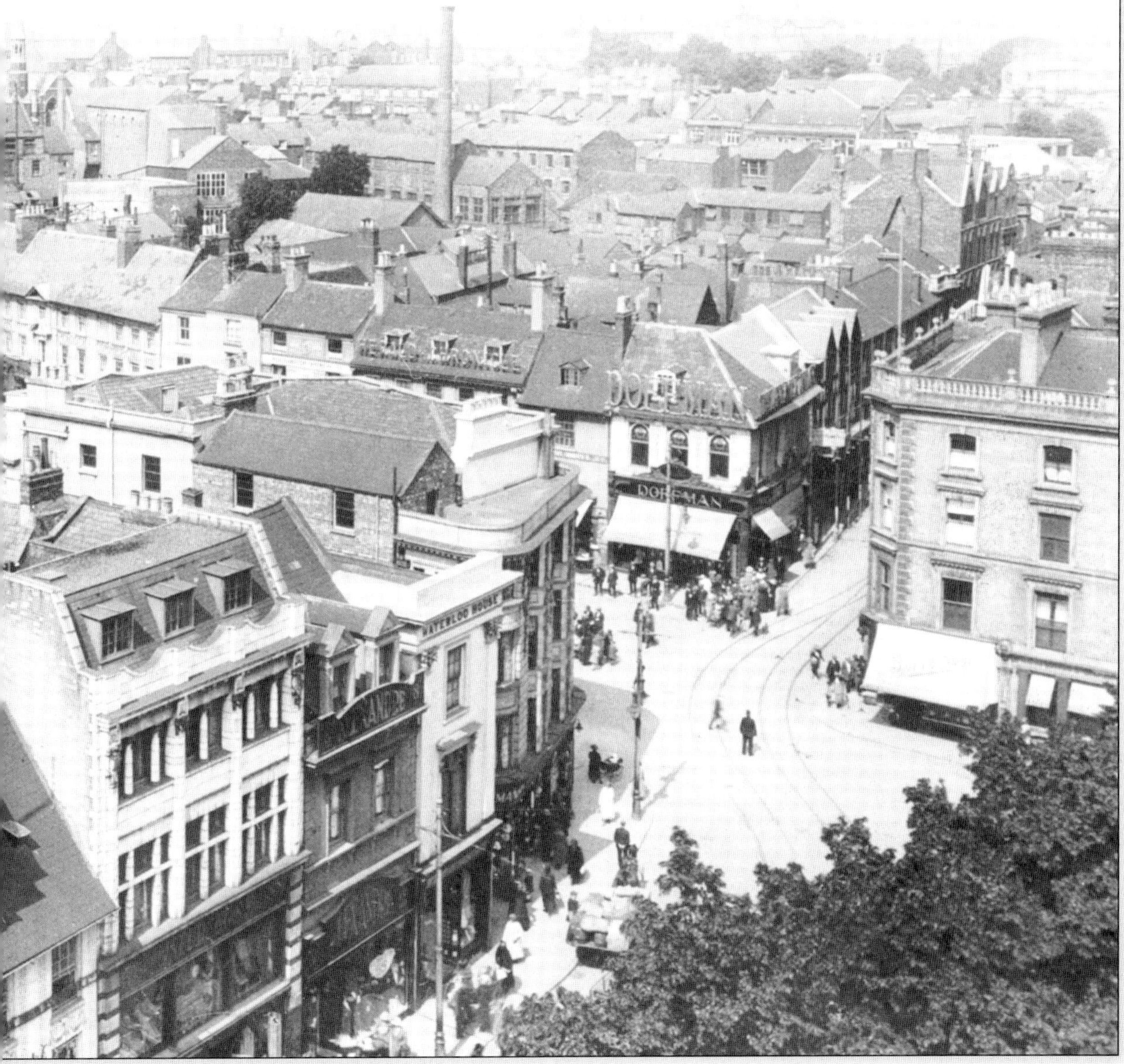

THE 1920S:

The Market Place, From the Tower of All Saints' Church 1922 72167

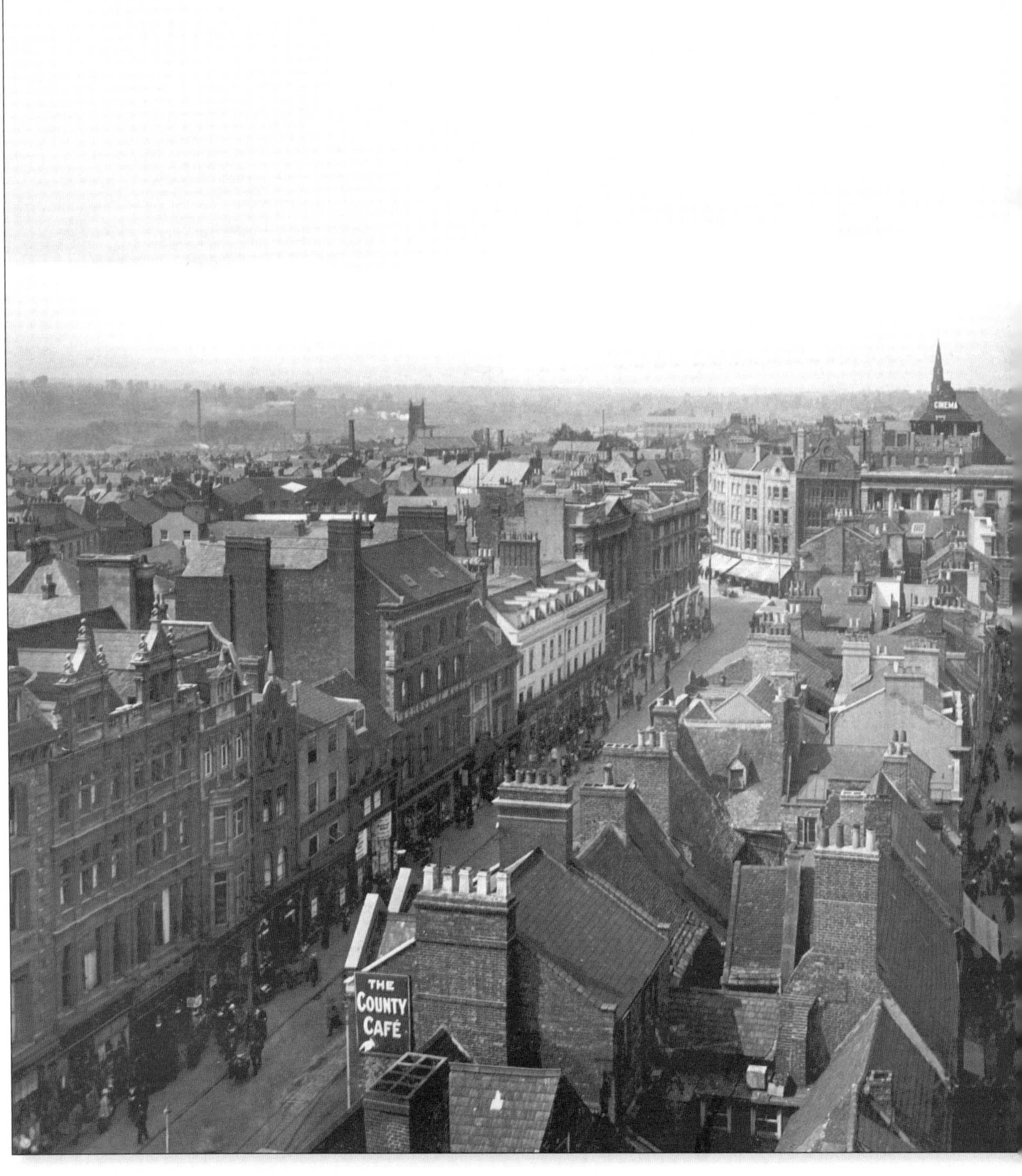

THE STREETS OF NORTHAMPTON

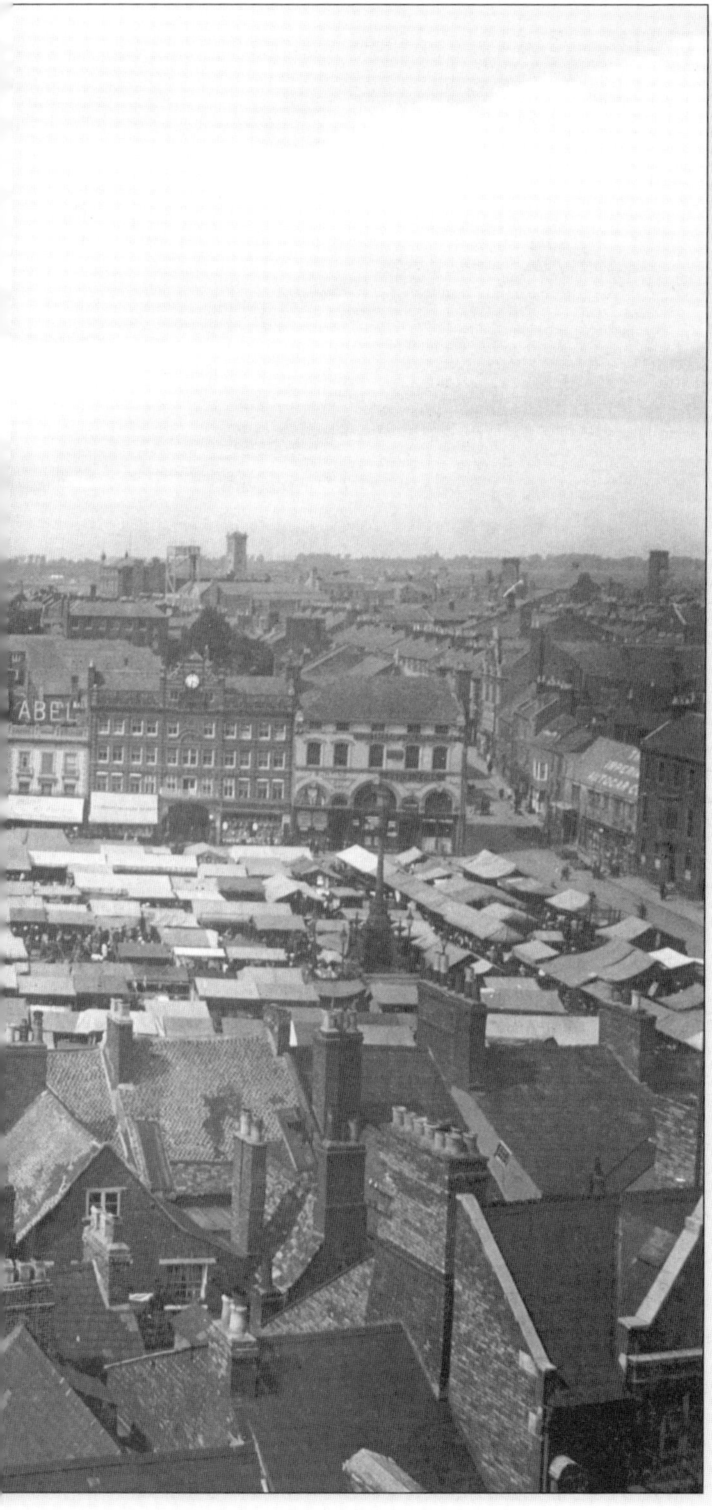

> *"Immense quantities of boots and shoes are still made for the supply of the army, the London market, and for exportation. A large trade is also carried on in the tanning and currying of leather. The breweries of Northampton are among the largest in the kingdom, and there are several important maltings and large flour mills. There are also some extensive iron foundries, and bricks and tiles are made to a considerable extent around the town."*
>
> BRABNER'S GAZETTEER OF ENGLAND AND WALES 1895

This third chapter gives a snapshot of Northampton soon after the First World War. The description from 1895 still held good, although the proportion of the town's population working in the shoe trade was declining: in the 1921 census, male shoemakers at 7,836 were down to 26% of the male workforce. The proportion was to decline further by 1930. However, the town had enjoyed both a good and a bad experience of the Great War. The demand for army boots was virtually insatiable, and in 1915 the town's factories were supplying over 140,000 pairs of boots to the French and Belgian armies alone. During the War the town produced over 23 million pairs for the armed forces, while the surrounding boot and shoe towns such as Kettering and Earls Barton produced a further 24 million pairs. Set against this splendid war effort the town lost many men in the trenches, a total of over 1,700 from the town from the 6,000 lost by the Northamptonshire Regiment. At the end of the War, the servicemen and women were royally feasted in Abington Park with trestle tables groaning under the weight of nine roast bullocks, 350 hams, 24,000 pastries and 20,000 pints of beer.

The town's main war memorial was built at the east end of All Saints' churchyard (N40058, pages 64-65). Designed by Sir Edwin Lutyens, who also designed the Cenotaph in Whitehall, it was unveiled by General Lord Horne on Armistice Day, 11 November, in 1926. The view of the Market Place below right, shows another First World War memorial, this time to an individual soldier, and one of considerable distinction. Lieutenant Colonel Edgar Mobbs DSO rose from the rank of Private to command the 7th Battalion of the Northamptonshire Regiment. He was killed in action in the Ypres Salient on 31 July 1917 aged 35, unusually young for such high rank. This remarkable man had been captain of Northampton (Rugby) Football Club, the 'Saints', from 1907-1913, and had played seven times for England. The memorial was unveiled in 1921, but was moved from the Market Place to Abington Square in 1931 (N40033, page 70), where it joined another war memorial.

During the 1920s the town expanded further, and the council embarked on an ambitious programme of building council houses for the workers, mostly semi-detached brick houses with three bedrooms. The estates were largely to the north and east of the town, including Abington, Far Cotton, Kingsley, Kingsthorpe and Dallington — much of these areas had been incorporated within the borough's boundaries in 1901.

The population of the town itself was now growing more slowly as people moved beyond its boundaries. Indeed, from 87,021 in 1901 the population only grew to 90,895 in 1921 and to 92,341 in 1931. Part of the cause of this slowdown is to be seen in several of the views in this chapter: the tramway. The Northampton Street Tramways Company was founded in 1880. The horse-drawn trams were a great success, and assisted the move into the new suburbs for all classes of townspeople. The town centre increased its proportion of non-residential uses, with only the poorest quarters showing population increases. In 1902 the Council exercised its option to buy the tramway system, which then went from strength to strength; it was extended further into the suburbs, both east and west of

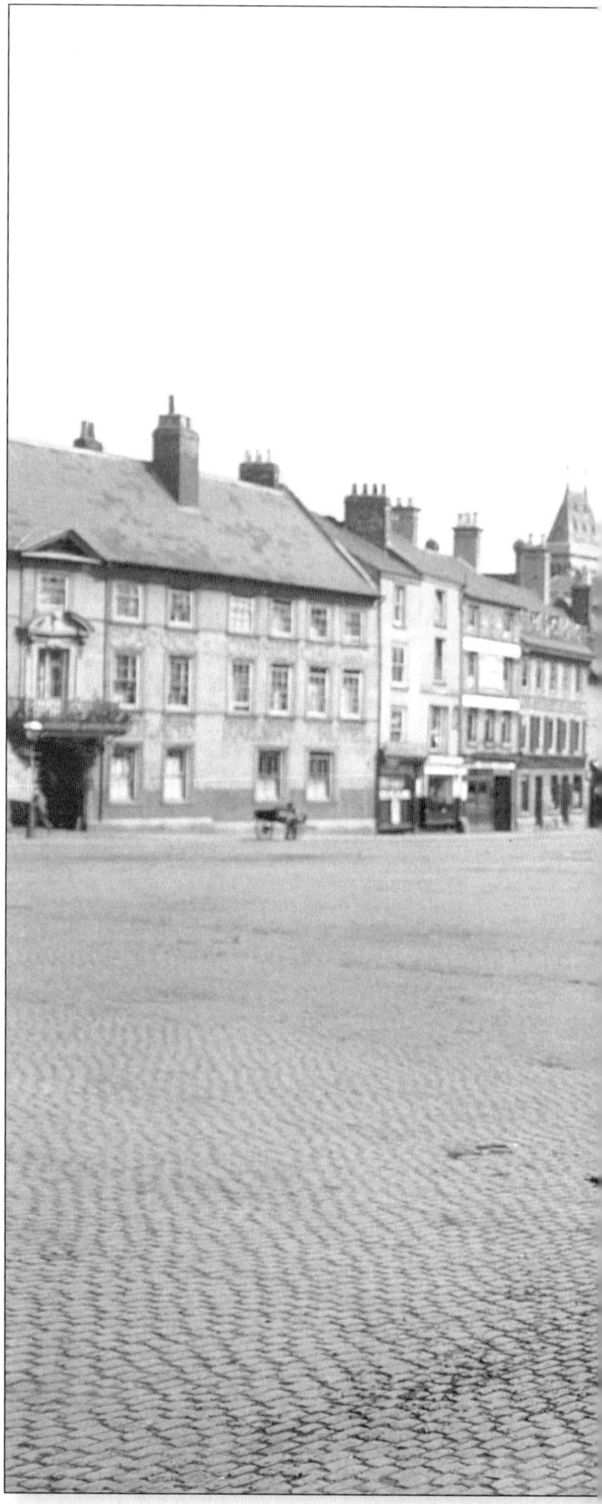

MARKET PLACE, LOOKING SOUTH 1922 *72169*

This photograph the view across this fine open space on a non-market day. In both we can see the elaborate lantern-topped fountain erected in 1863 to commemorate the marriage of the Prince of Wales, later Edward VII, to the Danish princess, Alexandra. Here we can also see the tower of the Guildhall and the cupola atop the tower of All Saints' Church.

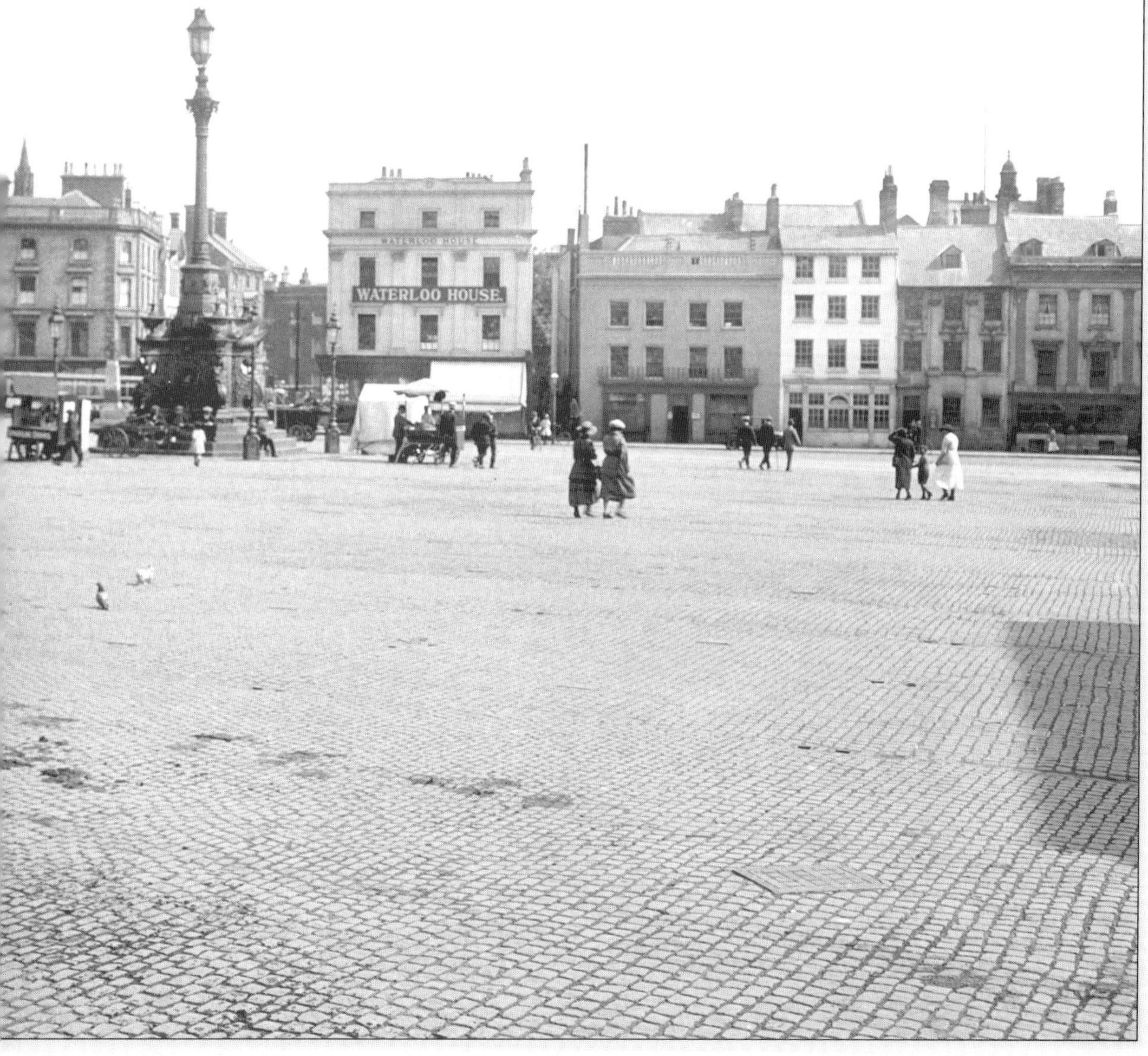

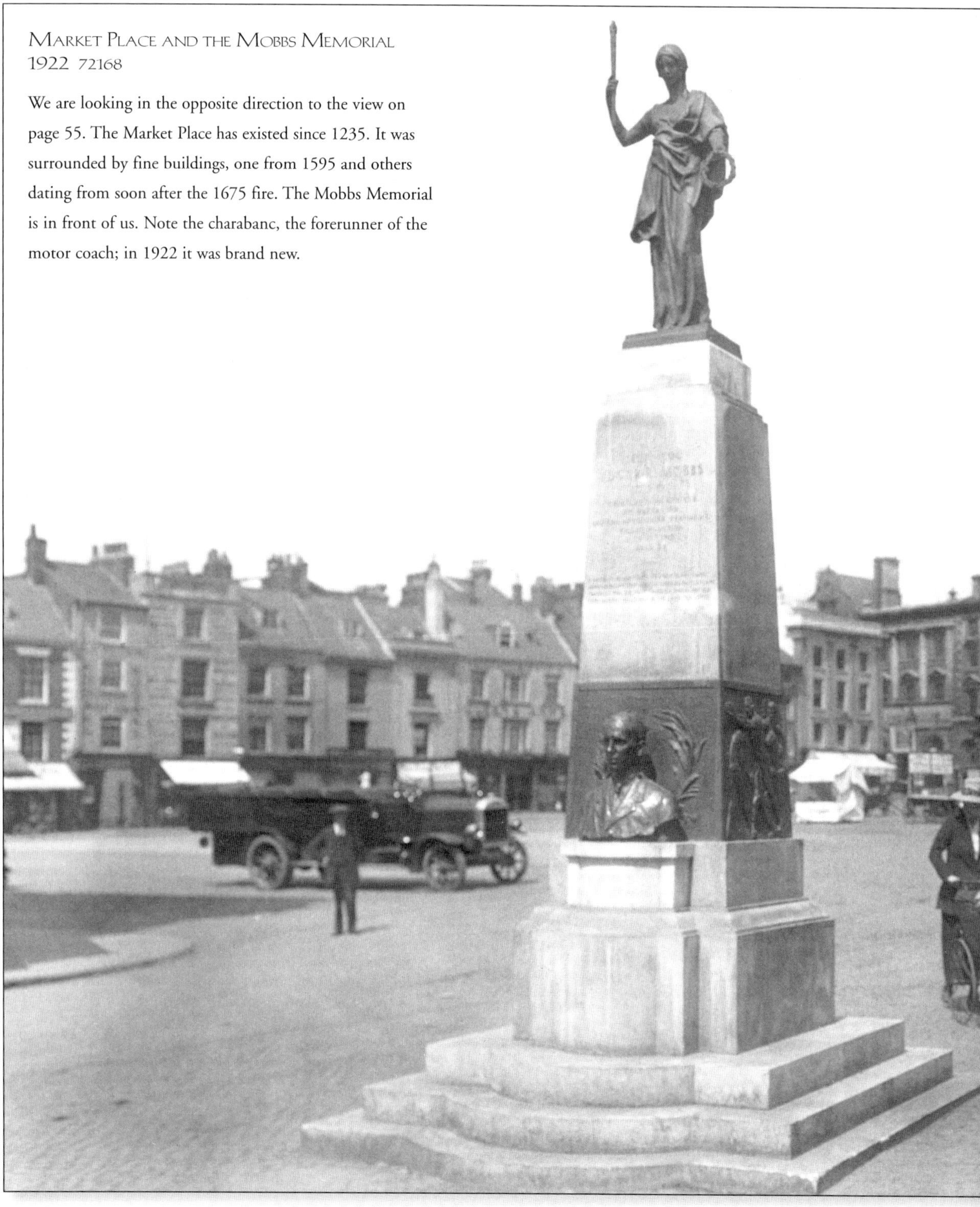

MARKET PLACE AND THE MOBBS MEMORIAL 1922 72168

We are looking in the opposite direction to the view on page 55. The Market Place has existed since 1235. It was surrounded by fine buildings, one from 1595 and others dating from soon after the 1675 fire. The Mobbs Memorial is in front of us. Note the charabanc, the forerunner of the motor coach; in 1922 it was brand new.

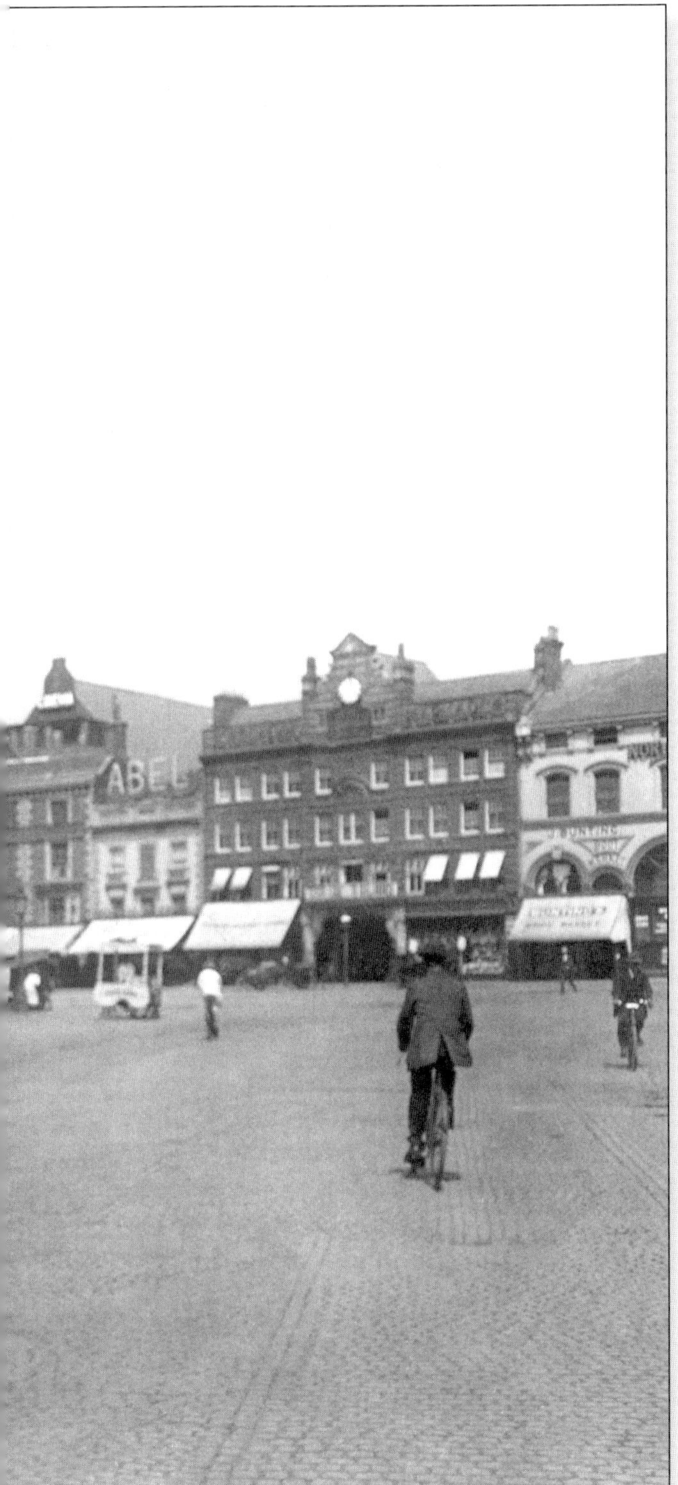

the town. The horse cars were replaced by electric trams in 1904. The new motive power allowed larger vehicles, and much to the sceptics' amazement, the corporation tramways made frequent profits.

The tramway system was gradually replaced by motor buses, and finally ceased to run in 1934, but the 1922 views, 72171 (page 58) and 72172 (page 60) show the tracks and their overhead electricity supply lines. The view in Gold Street (72176, pages 62-63) best shows the cable support standards with their metal scrollwork supporting the cable arms. Two views, one in The Drapery (72174, pages 62) and one in Abington Street, pages 60-61, show tram cars, while two also show cyclists riding between the tracks: a somewhat hazardous operation. Motor buses were introduced in 1923. They initially appeared on routes where trams could not easily be provided, and rapidly became popular. To the passenger, their pneumatic tyres and upholstered seats were infinitely preferable to the rattletrap trams with their plain wooden benches.

It is striking in these 1922 views how few cars and motor vehicles are to be seen. Indeed, in 1921 there were under 6,000 road fund licences issued for the town, and most of these were for commercial vehicles. The number increased to 16,000 by 1930, with a higher proportion of private cars. This was the dawn of the age of the private motor car, with the famous Austin Seven and other 'economy' cars bringing car ownership within the reach of the lower middle classes — the first Austin Seven was produced in 1923, a year after the views in this chapter. The effects of motor transport will be seen more clearly in the next chapter, although this only takes the story into the 1950s, which was before the late 20th century explosion in car ownership and vastly increased road freight as the railways declined.

THE 1920S:

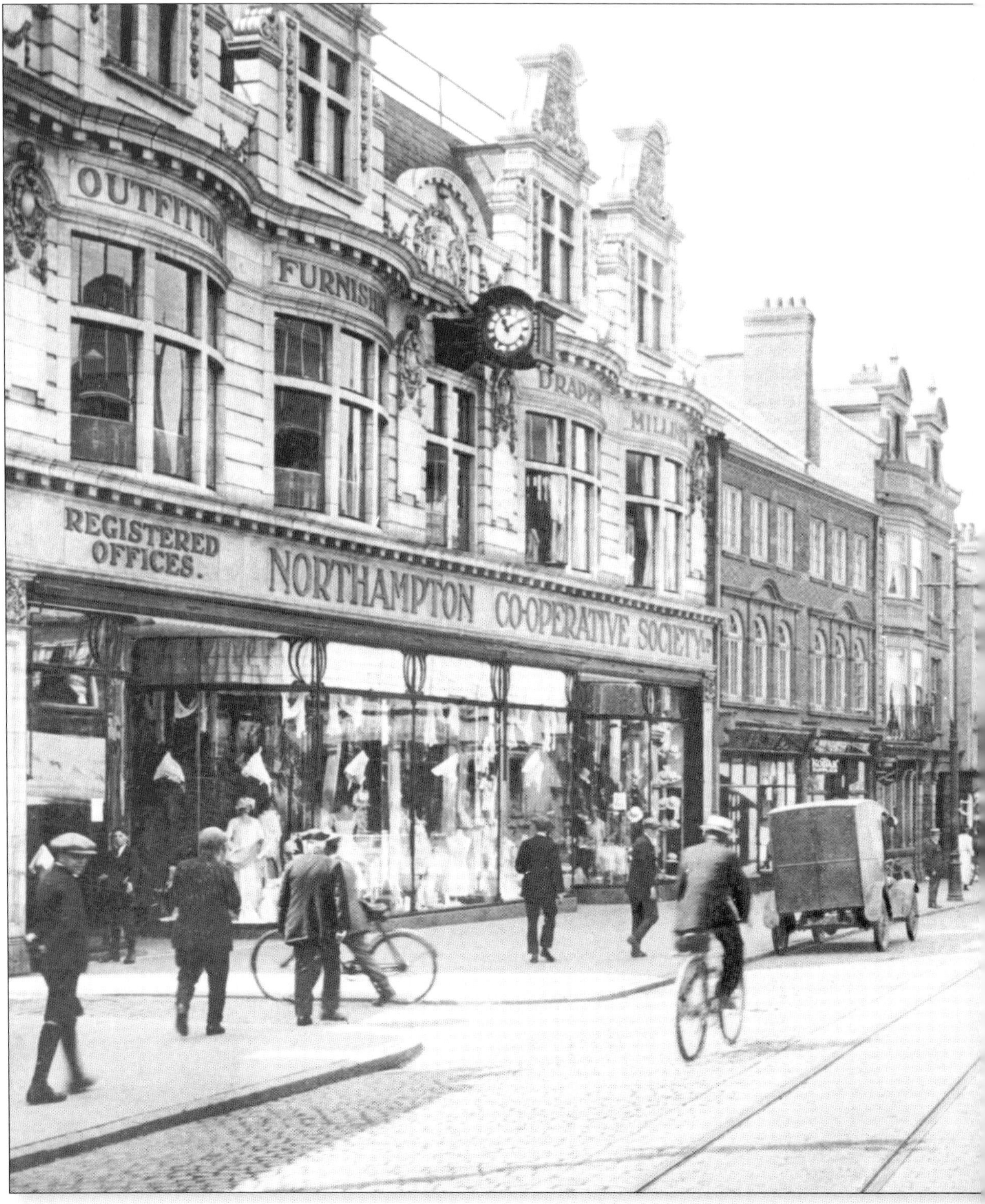
OUTFITTIN
FURNISHI
DRAPER
MILLIN
REGISTERED OFFICES.
NORTHAMPTON CO-OPERATIVE SOCIETY LTD

ABINGTON STREET, LOOKING SOUTH-WEST 1922 72171

The tramway runs along the street, although the overhead cables are virtually washed out by the photograph's exposure. Note the rather fine and elaborate late 19th-century facade of the Northampton Co-operative Society store, which was replaced in 1938 by an Art Deco building — it still survives.

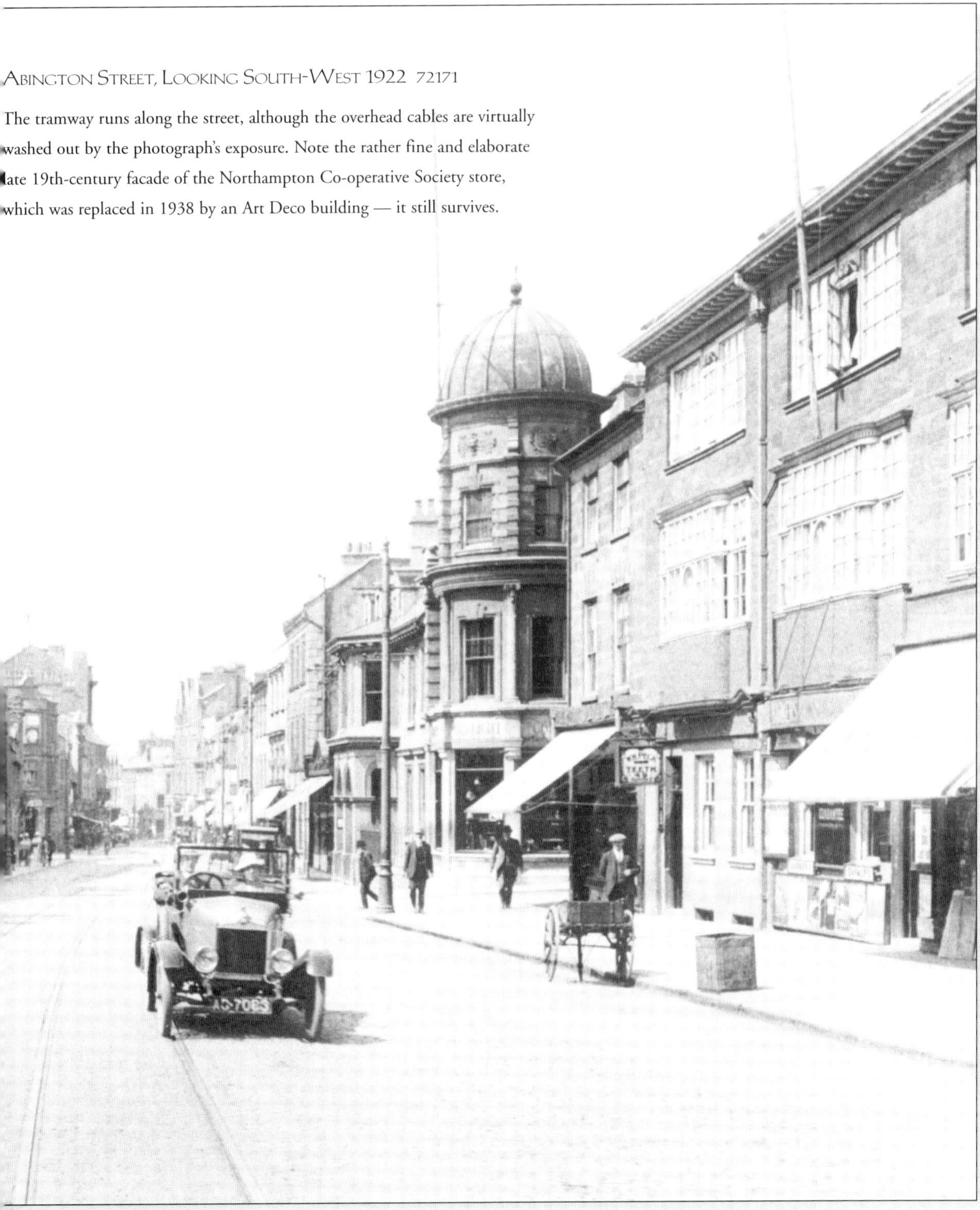

THE 1920S:

ABINGTON STREET AND NOTRE DAME HIGH SCHOOL 1922 72172

Here we can actually see a tramcar. This is passing the forbidding brickwork of the old Notre Dame High School, which was built in 1871 as a school and convent run by the Sisters of Notre Dame de Namur.

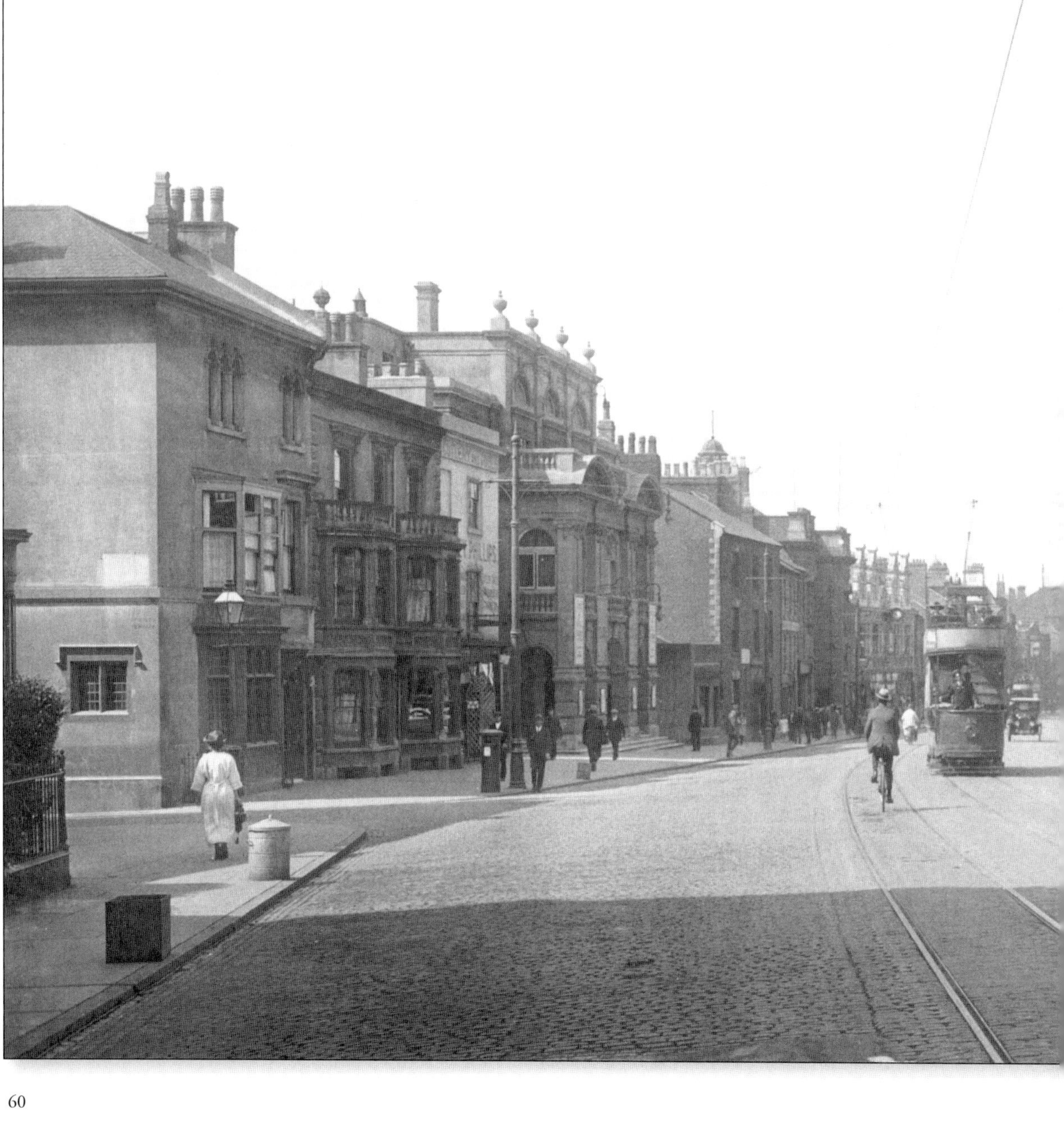

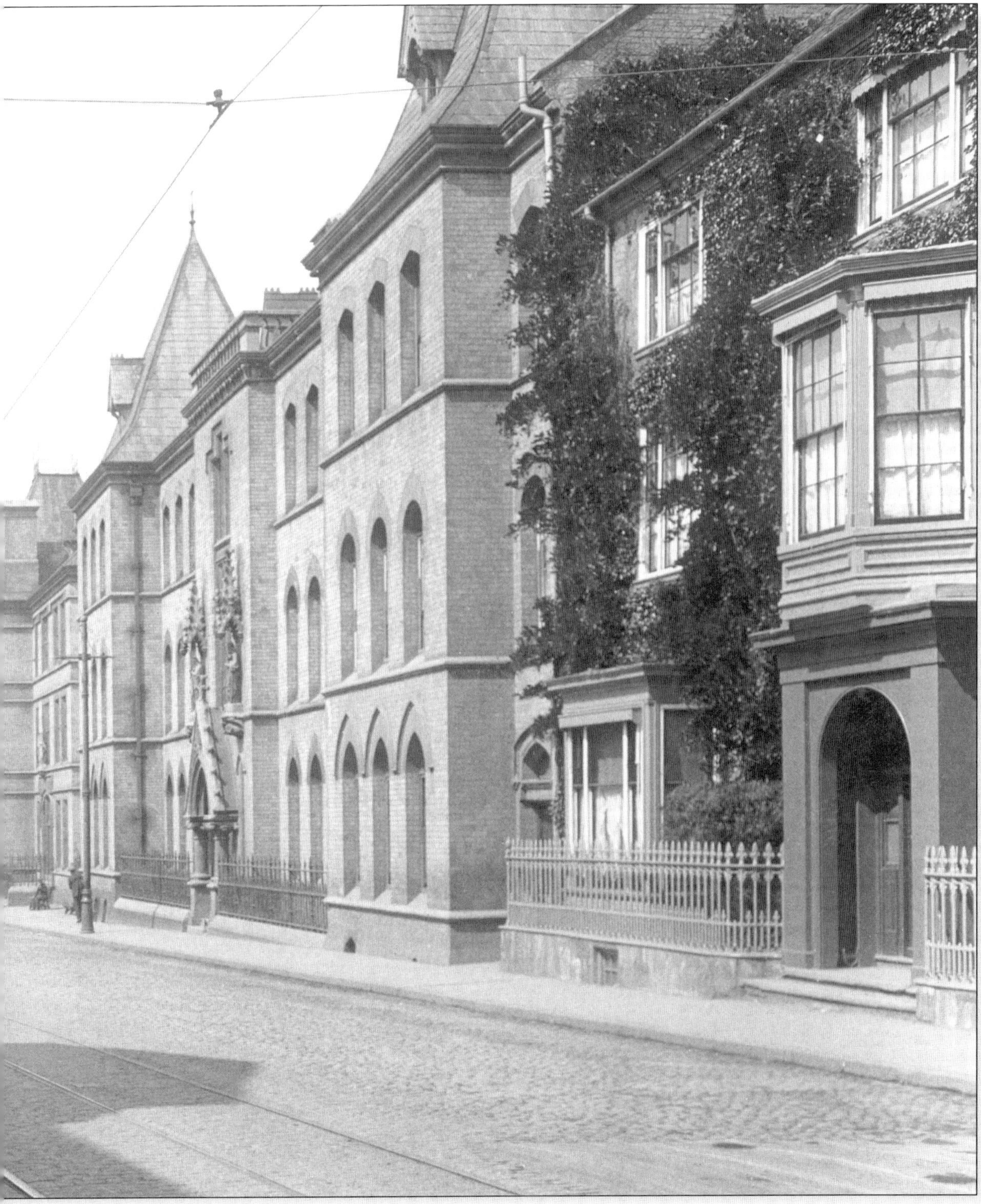

THE 1920s:

Right: HAZELRIGG HOUSE AND MARE FAIR 1922 72176

This view is taken from beside the 17th-century pre-fire stone survivor, Hazelrigg House, looking east along the tram tracks, with the road widening towards Horse Market. All the buildings on the left have recently been replaced (in 2002) by the Sol Central complex, which includes an Ibis Hotel.

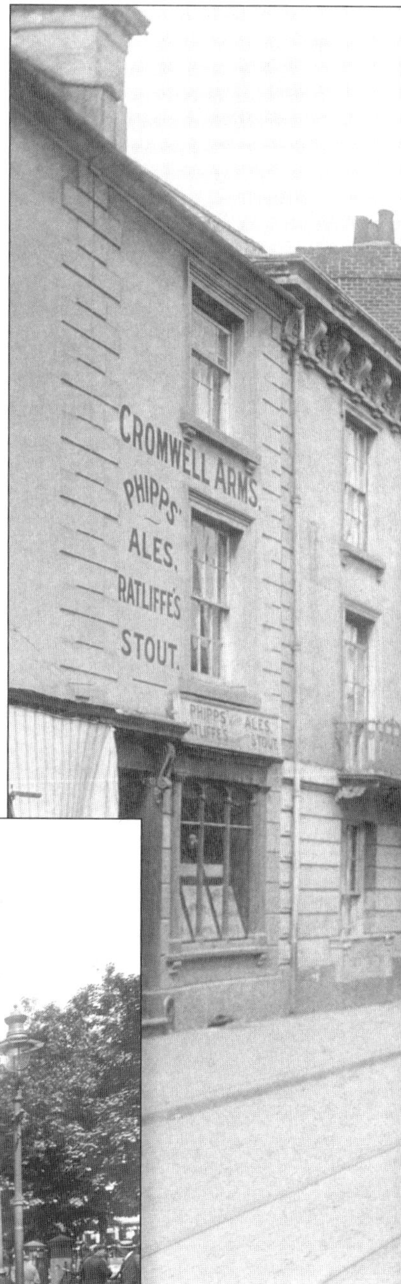

Below: THE DRAPERY 1922 72174

We are looking past the trees in front of All Saints'. The Drapery has some fine commercial buildings past which the trams rattle. Many years ago it was known as the Glovery, once an important leather industry in the town before boots and shoes swept all before them. On the left the road leads past H Samuel, the jewellers, into Gold Street, formerly Goldsmith Street, which leads west to Mare Fair.

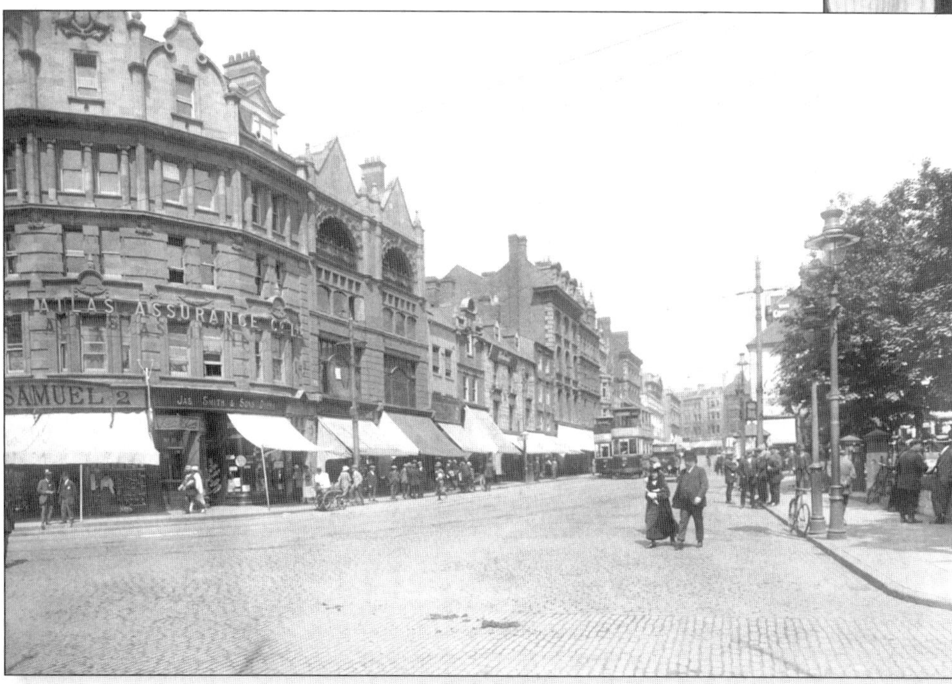

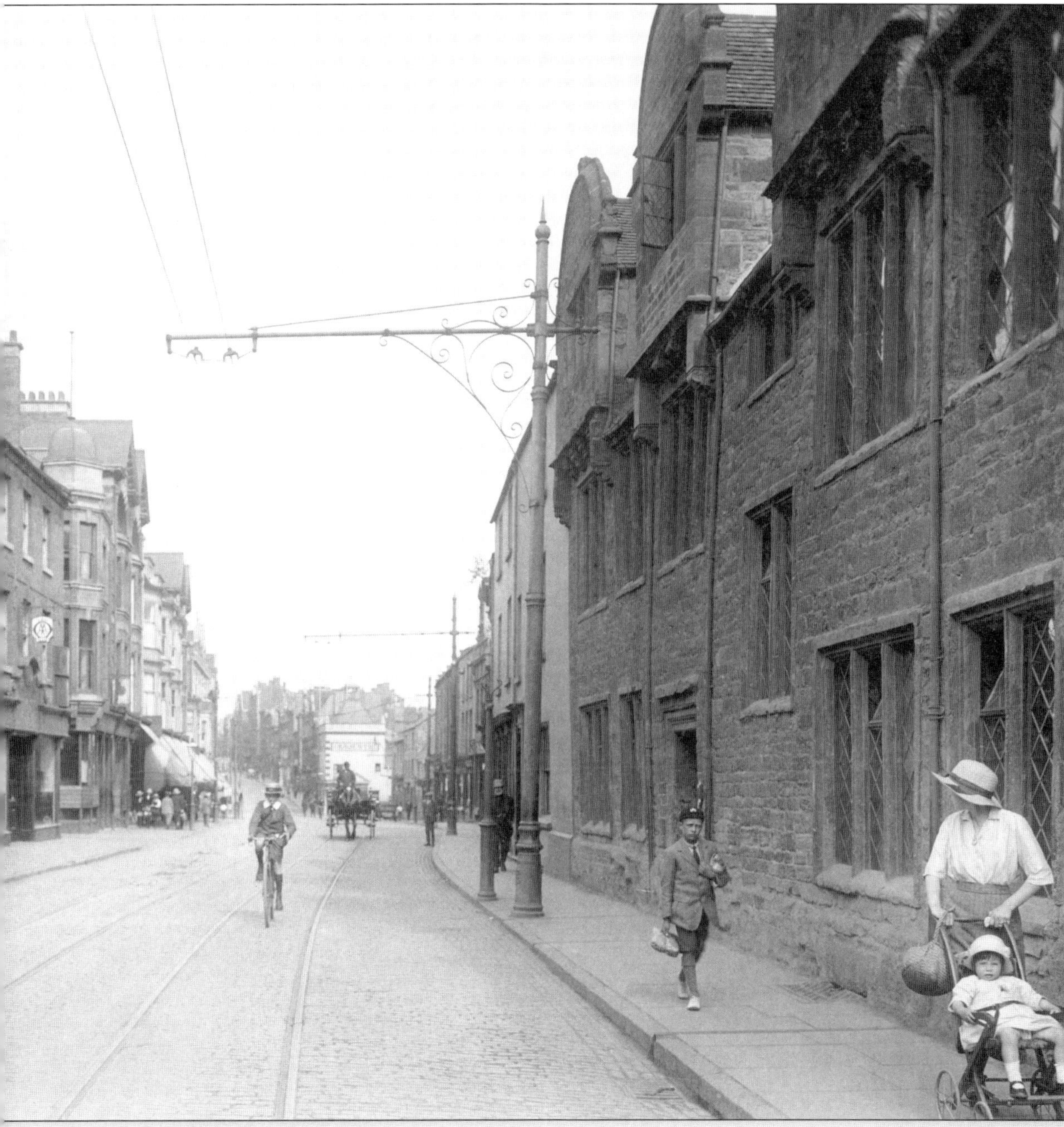

THE TOWN AFTER THE SECOND WORLD WAR

The photographs accompanying this chapter take us on a tour of the town in the 1950s, the decade immediately prior to vast changes in the town. Large numbers of good buildings were demolished, and replaced mostly by bad ones; this was an era when it was the received wisdom that the only way of getting out of the economic doldrums was to rebuild and redevelop. A policy of emptying the baby out with the bath water was vigorously pursued, and some truly appalling buildings appeared. I will just mention as an example the Moat House Hotel of 1971-72 in Horse Market: it takes a lot of beating, particularly as it is now painted in in-your-face colours. The 1970s Grosvenor Centre on the north side of Market Place eliminated an entire street, Newland, and the Greyfriars Bus Station beyond is an extraordinary building.

However, all this was in the future at the time when the views in this chapter were taken, so this is a record of a Midlands town before a major expansion and reconstruction programme started, a town in which small brick factory buildings and foundries co-existed with the shops, houses and offices, and smells wafted across the town from the tanneries and the breweries. This was before much of the town's fabric surrendered to the motor car and lorry, and before the inner ring road; this, among other urban crimes, turned the old Horse Market, Broad Street and Gas Street into a dual carriageway cutting Mare Fair off from the main town centre. Fortunately, the town had enough character and enough density of historic buildings to weather the storm with much of its character intact. This chapter, as a consequence, looks at the town as it was half a century ago: a little drab and shabby, and still gripped in post-war austerity — and very much an historical record now.

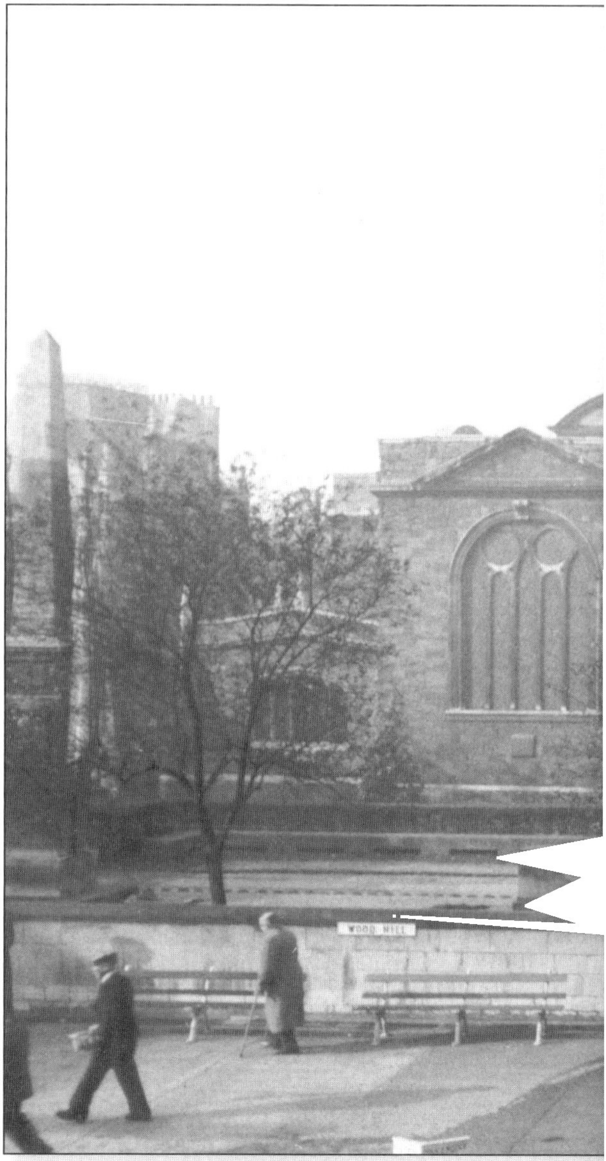

In the 1950s, Northampton was, of course, blissfully unaware of the changes the 1960s would wreak upon the town. In 1965 it was announced in parliament that Northampton, along with Peterborough and Ipswich, was to become a 'New Town' to accommodate London overspill. Eventually the Northampton Development Corporation was established in 1968. A Master Plan was produced in 1969, and work started on new housing and industrial estates and centres, initially to the east and south of the town. The census shows the effects of this expansion. There was near stagnation in the 1950s, when the population rose by only a thousand between 1951 and 1961 to 105,421. In the 1960s it increased by nearly a third to 133,800 in 1971, and accelerated to 157,217 by 1981, roughly a 50% increase in twenty years.

These figures give some idea of the effects of the changes which took place after the decade celebrated in this chapter, the 1950s. Mind you, there had been dramatic 'progress'

ALL SAINTS' CHURCH, FROM THE EAST c1960 N40058

Since the comparable 1922 view, Sir Edwin Lutyens' War Memorial of 1926 dominates the view west from Wood Hill. Built in the east part of All Saints' churchyard as a memorial garden facing Wood Hill, it consists of two obelisks with an altar in between. The wall in front incorporates the steps down to underground public conveniences. The low chapel on the far left of the church is the War Memorial chapel added in 1920.

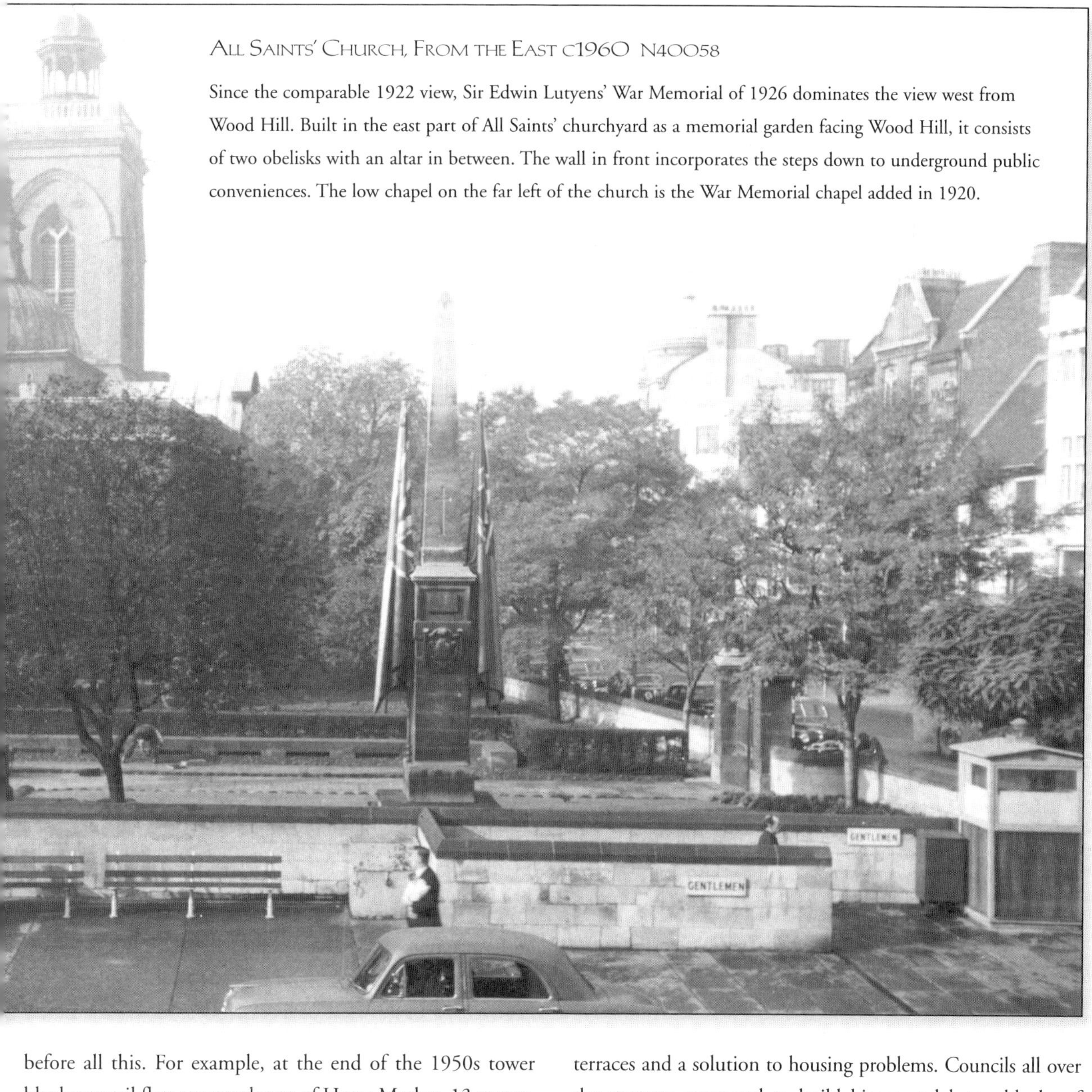

before all this. For example, at the end of the 1950s tower block council flats appeared west of Horse Market, 13-storey-high blocks of flats to replace artisan terraces. This was a radically different response to housing needs to the traditional brick-built semi-detached and terraced council houses built in large numbers during the 1950s.

Now discredited, at that time tower blocks seemed to offer a brave new world away from cramped streets of artisan terraces and a solution to housing problems. Councils all over the country competed to build bigger and better blocks of council flats. Northampton, however, did not have the same sort of housing problems as, say, Nottingham, with its acres of cramped slums. In the end, relatively few council flat tower blocks were constructed in Northampton, though at the time they were seen as evidence of a progressive and forward-looking county borough council.

THE TOWN AFTER THE SECOND WORLD WAR

Above Right: MARKET PLACE, LOOKING SOUTH-WEST c1955 N40053

In 1955, the fountain of 1863 erected to commemorate the wedding of Prince Edward, later Edward VII, and Princess Alexandra still had a few years to go before being declared unsafe; it was demolished in 1962. The south side buildings are still intact to the left of the fountain.

Below Left: MARKET PLACE, LOOKING NORTH-WEST c1955 N40026

The buildings on the left, the west side of the Market Place, mostly survive today, apart from the two at the far left. Unlike a French market square, the south and west side of Northampton's market place in particular have a delightful informality and physical variety, with no building the same as its neighbour.

Below Right: MARKET PLACE, NORTH SIDE c1950 N40009

This is very much an archive shot of the vanished 1950s town. This north side of the market place is now all demolished, including the grandiose Emporium Arcade of 1901 and the Mercury and Herald offices to its right and the three buildings to its left. Much of it went for the Grosvenor Centre shopping malls, which also obliterated an entire street, Newland, to the right of the Mercury and Herald offices.

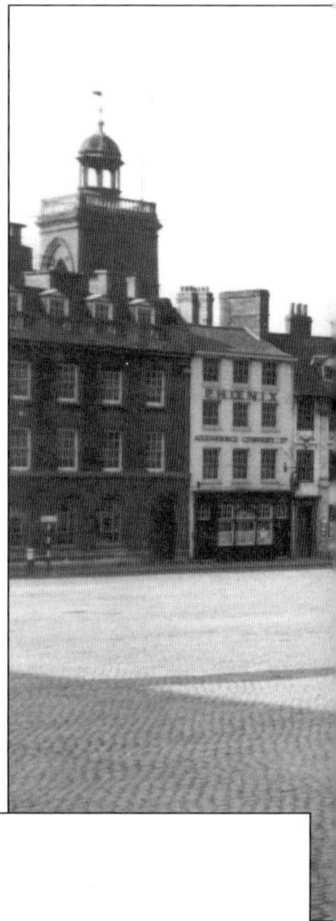

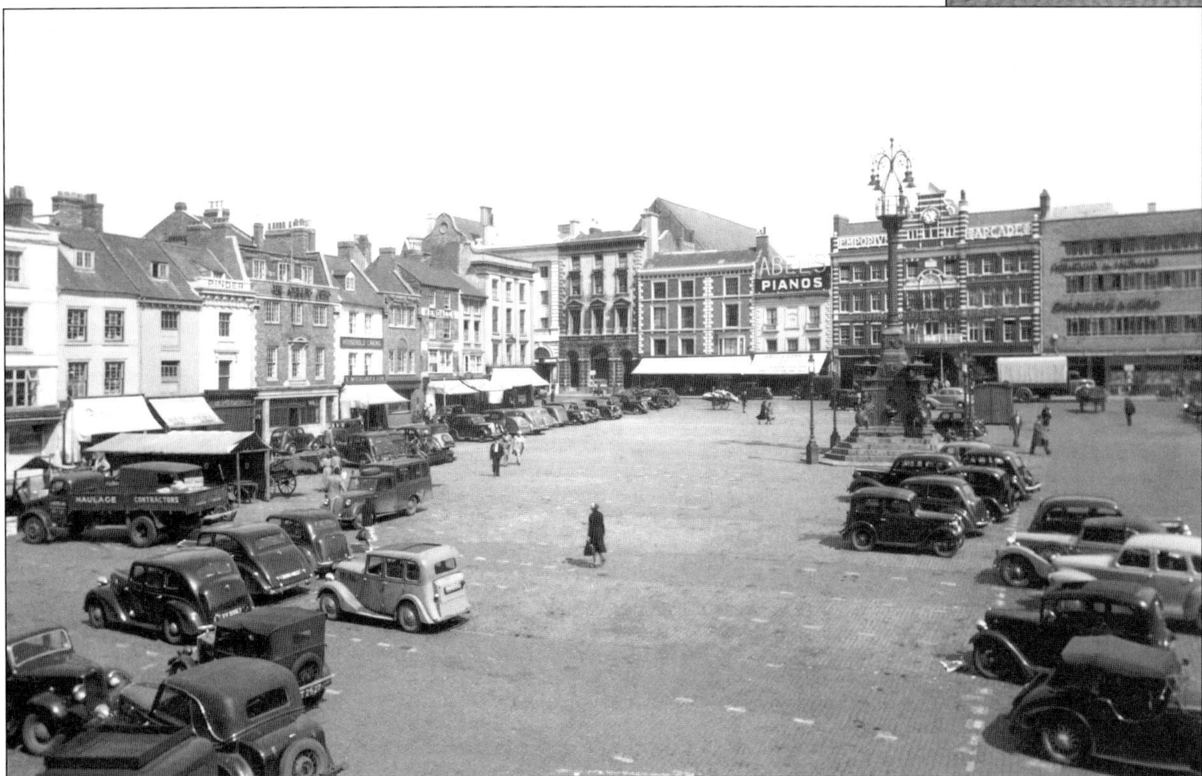

THE TOWN AFTER THE SECOND WORLD WAR

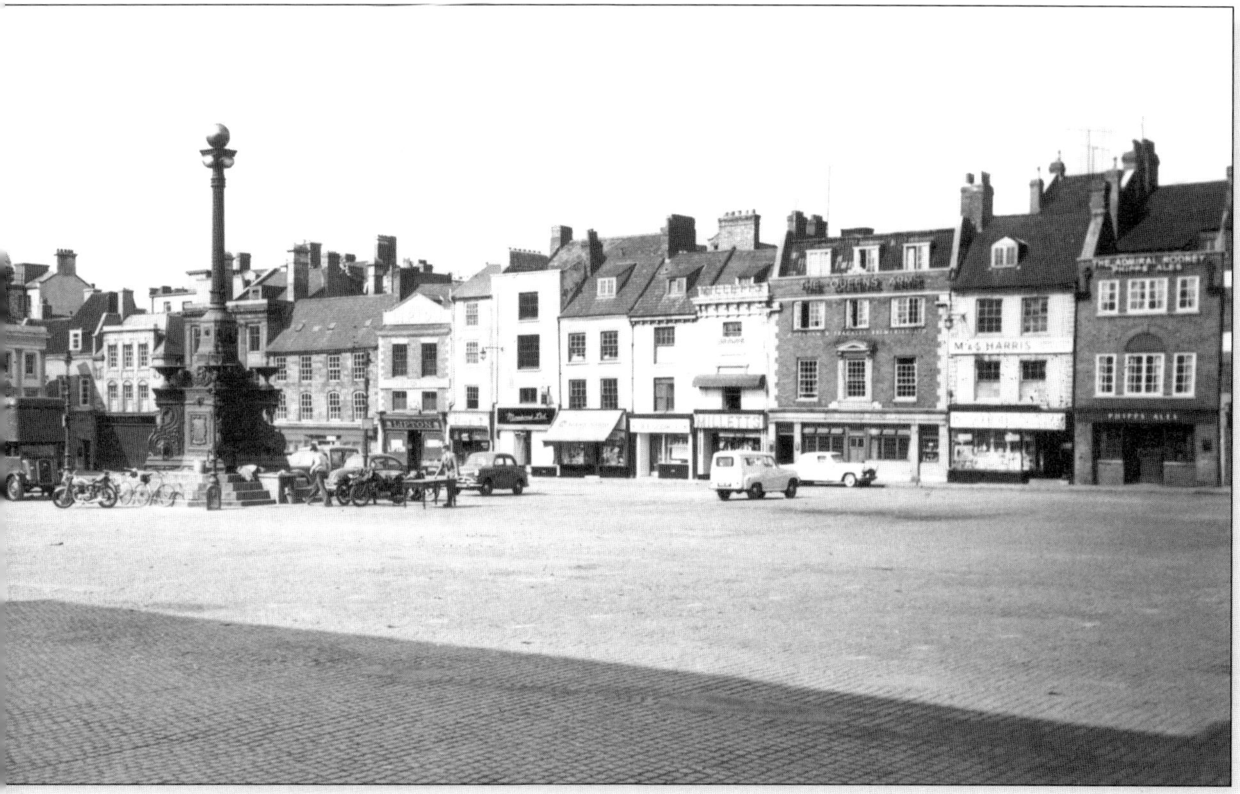

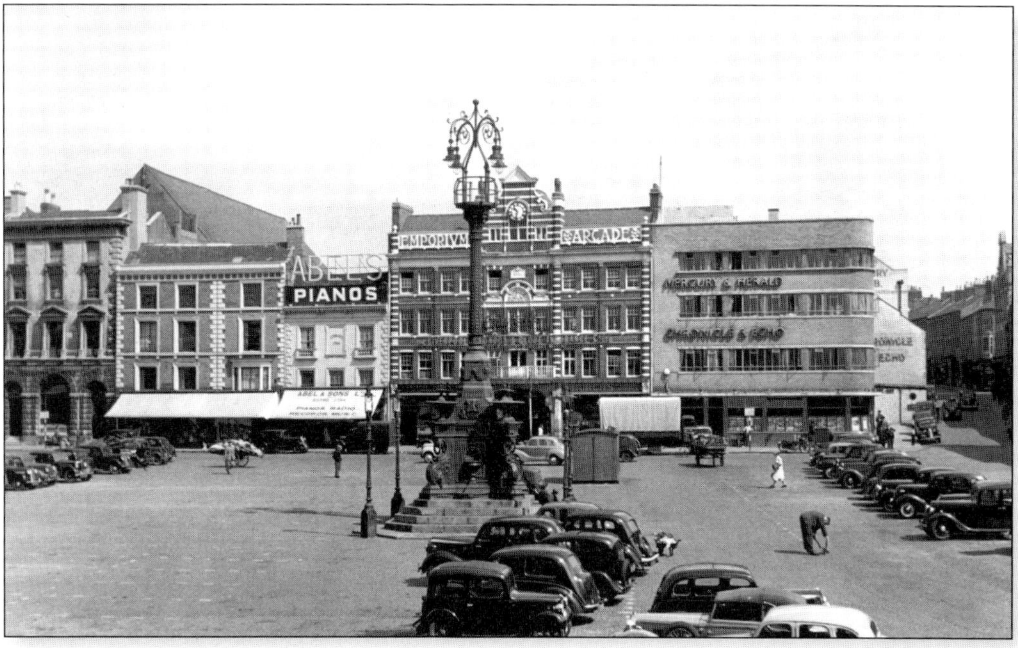

THE TOWN AFTER THE SECOND WORLD WAR

However, as the views in this chapter show, the town centre had relatively little replacement building in the 1950s. Indeed, around the Market Place, virtually the only new building was the Mercury and Herald building on the corner of Newland, and most of the post-1914 buildings in these 1950s views went up in the 1920s and 1930s. This is not the place to detail the extensive demolitions and reconstructions that afflicted the town centre to produce the vast Grosvenor Centre, which opened in 1965. Several key buildings in the Market Place were lost, to be replaced by mediocre modern panelled-front offices or pastiche brick ones, or the drab buildings that replaced the Notre Dame High School.

MARKET PLACE, LOOKING NORTH-EAST c1950 N40008

This view shows the Georgian Peacock Hotel (right), shamefully demolished in 1959. Beyond the (surviving) house with the Gothick oriel window is the Welsh House, white-painted and with a shop front. This dates from 1595. It survived the 1675 fire and was rebuilt in the 1970s, its long-lost gabled dormers restored.

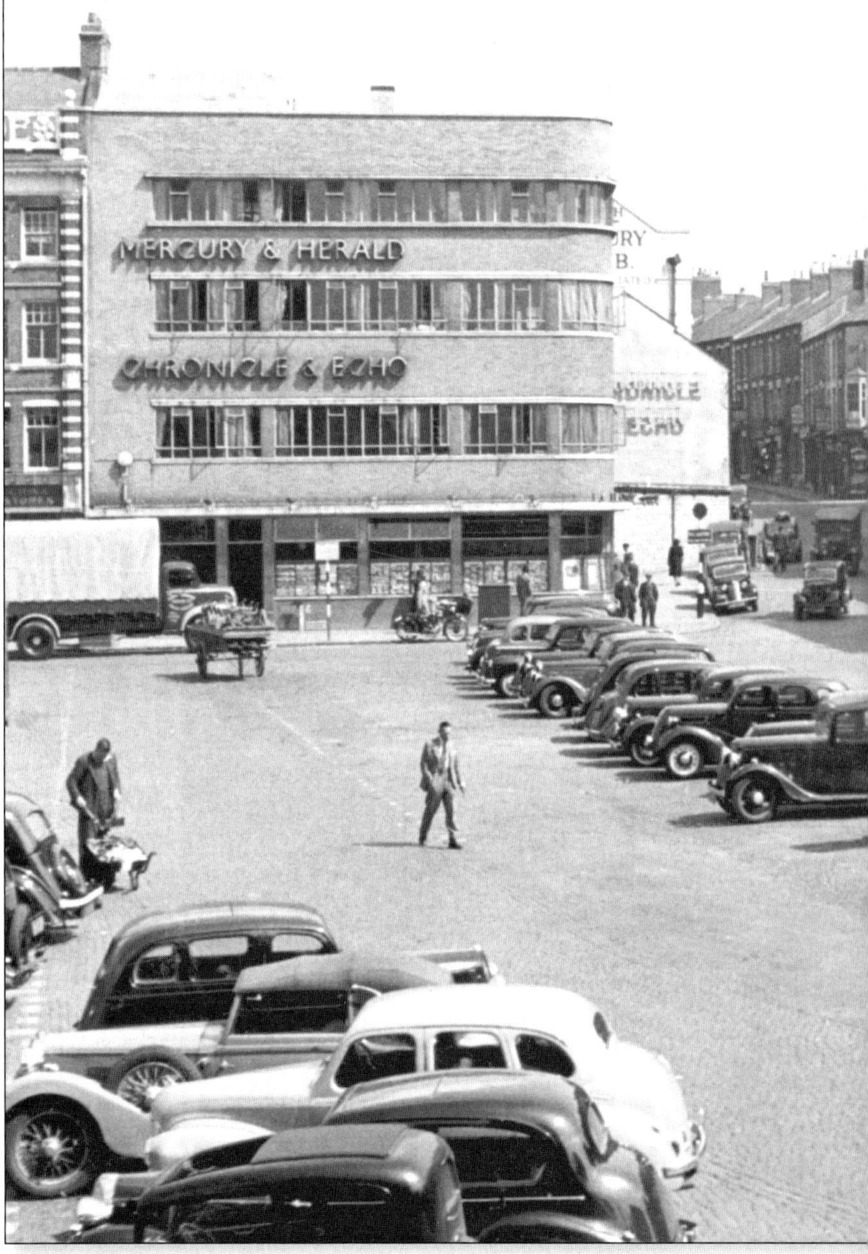

THE TOWN AFTER THE SECOND WORLD WAR

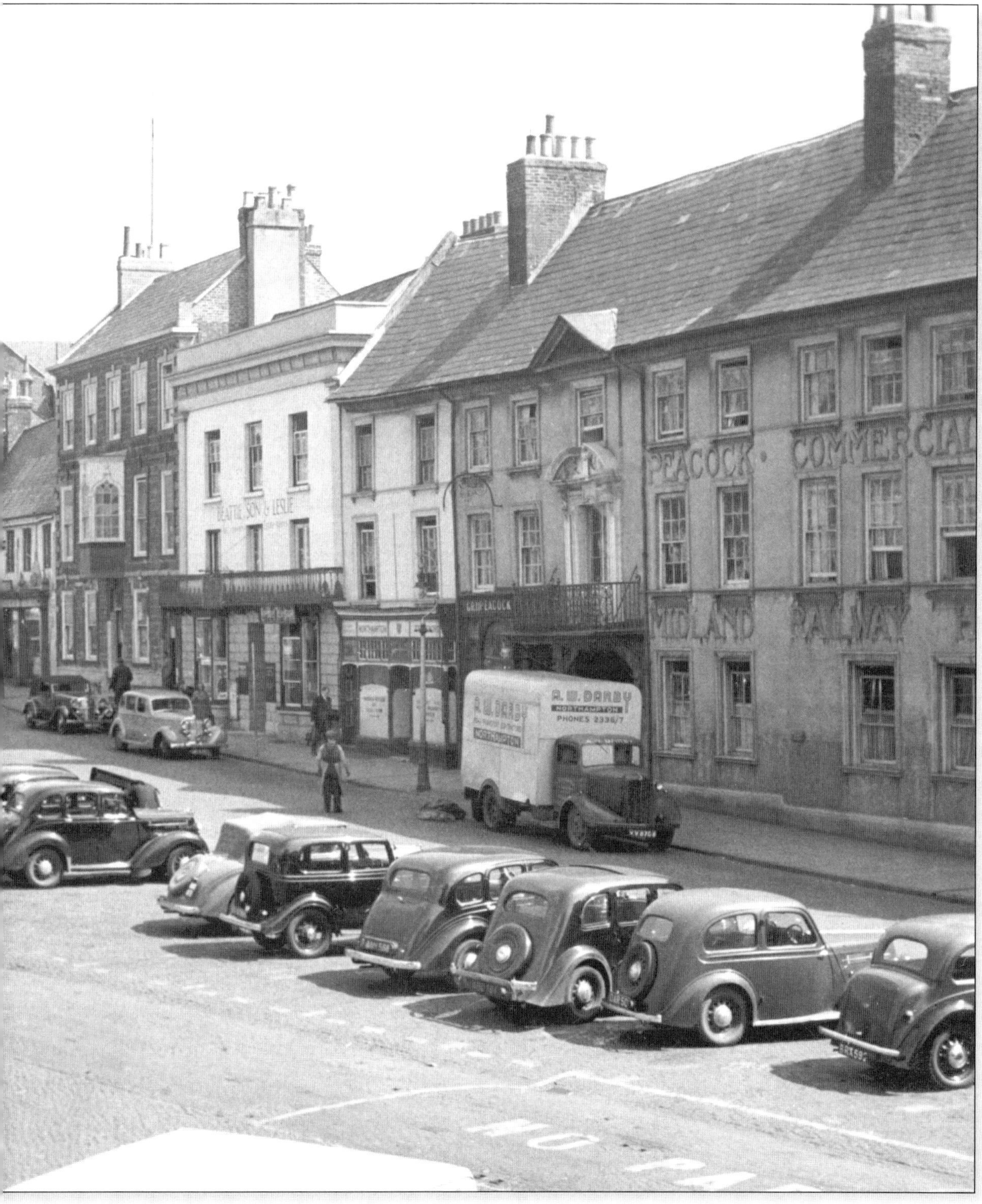

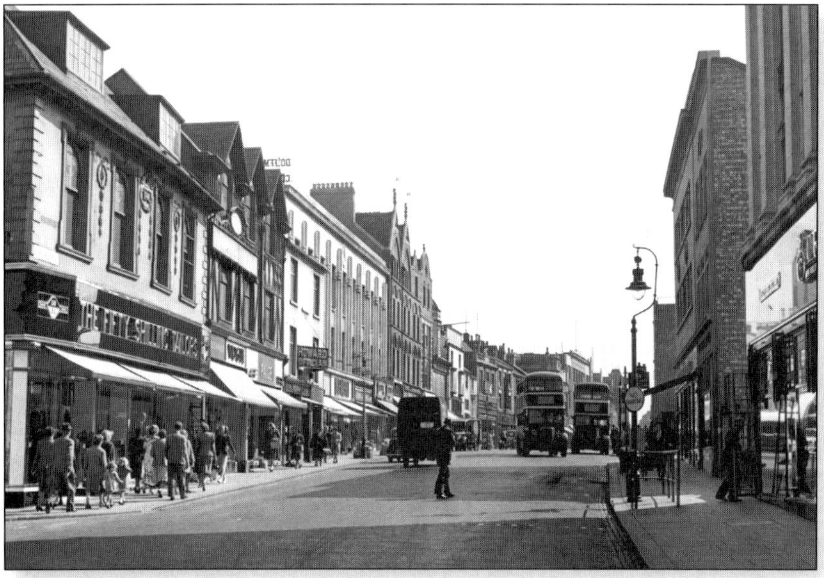

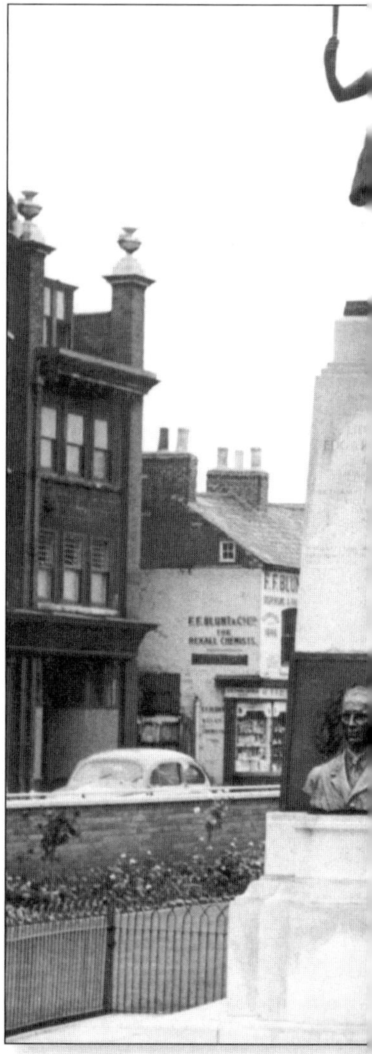

Above Left: ABINGTON STREET, FROM MARKET PLACE c1955 N40002

Below Left: ABINGTON STREET, NOTRE DAME HIGH SCHOOL c1955 N40060

These two views show Abington Street from each end. Above we are looking from the Market Place. On the left a 1677 building houses the Fifty Shilling Tailors, then a great rival of Burton's on the opposite side of the road. Beyond is an Art Deco 1930s front, now an Adams store. Below shows two buildings in their last years. On the right is the Notre Dame High School's long severe brick frontage with its slated pyramid turrets, which was demolished in 1975, and the New Theatre stands opposite with the four urns on its parapet. Abington Street, as the main shopping street, suffered more rebuilding since the 1960s than other streets of the town centre.

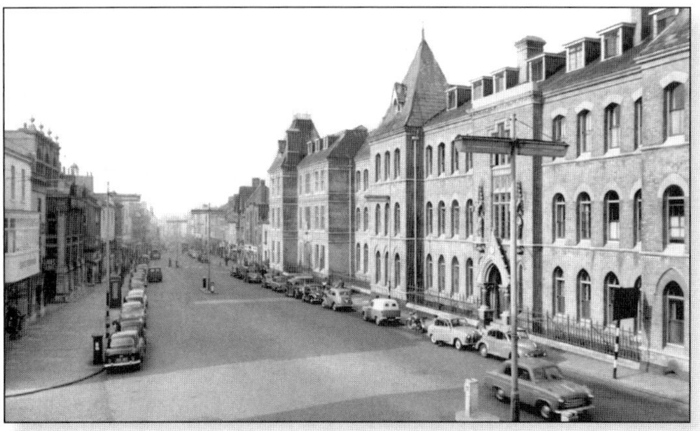

THE TOWN AFTER THE SECOND WORLD WAR

ABINGTON SQUARE AND THE MOBBS MEMORIAL C1955 N40033

We are looking west towards the town centre; behind is the 1937 War Memorial Loggia, with a wall listing the names of Northampton men who fell in the two world wars, and in front is the Edgar Mobbs Memorial, relocated here from the Market Place in 1931. Beyond is a statue to Charles Bradlaugh (1833-91), the Northampton freethinker, atheist and, eventually MP for the town. Elected in 1880, he refused to swear his oath 'so help me God', and was only allowed to take his seat in 1886.

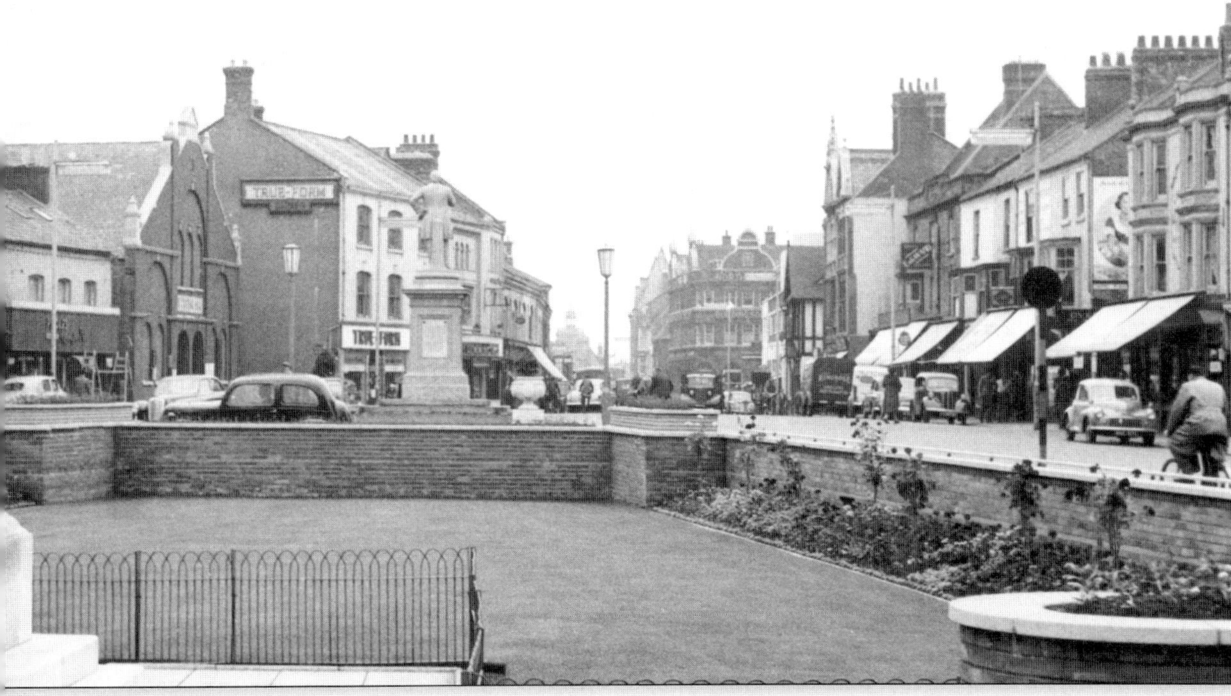

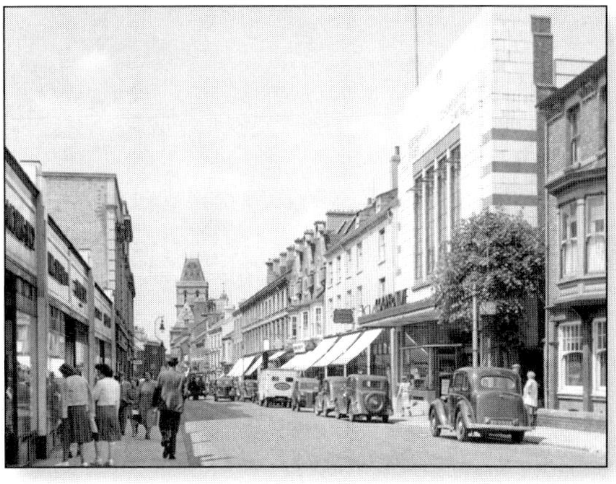

Right: ST GILES STREET C1955 N40015

This view down St Giles Street has the Guildhall tower in the distance and the 1938 Co-op on the right, a building in Art Deco style. The terrace with the deeply-shadowed eaves in the middle distance is the 17th-century Massingberd Charity Gift buildings, rebuilt in 1864.

THE TOWN AFTER THE SECOND WORLD WAR

Our 1950s photo tour now moves west of Market Place to views in Mercers Row. The first looks north-east from an upper window of Palmer's, the hand-tailored clothes shop, past the portico of All Saints' Church into Mercers Row, past the Adam-style 1920s Westminster Bank with its domed corner turret, now the Nationwide. The second view, N40001, page 74, looks west along Mercers Row past the Geisha, formerly the Old Oak Café; it was built in 1909 and is now a Tony and Guy hairdressers. All Saints' stands on the left in its tree-lined churchyard.

Suffice it to say that fortunately enough of the town's pre-1960 fabric remains to make the present town centre well worth close inspection. There is no doubt that pedestrianisation of much of Abington Street and the retention of Market Place as a real market place have helped give the town back to the people after disastrous flirtations with the mighty motor car and its demand for ring roads. But even so, the views in this chapter represent a period of calm before the storm of change, and are very much an archive of a bustling town which now has a population of 100,000 people.

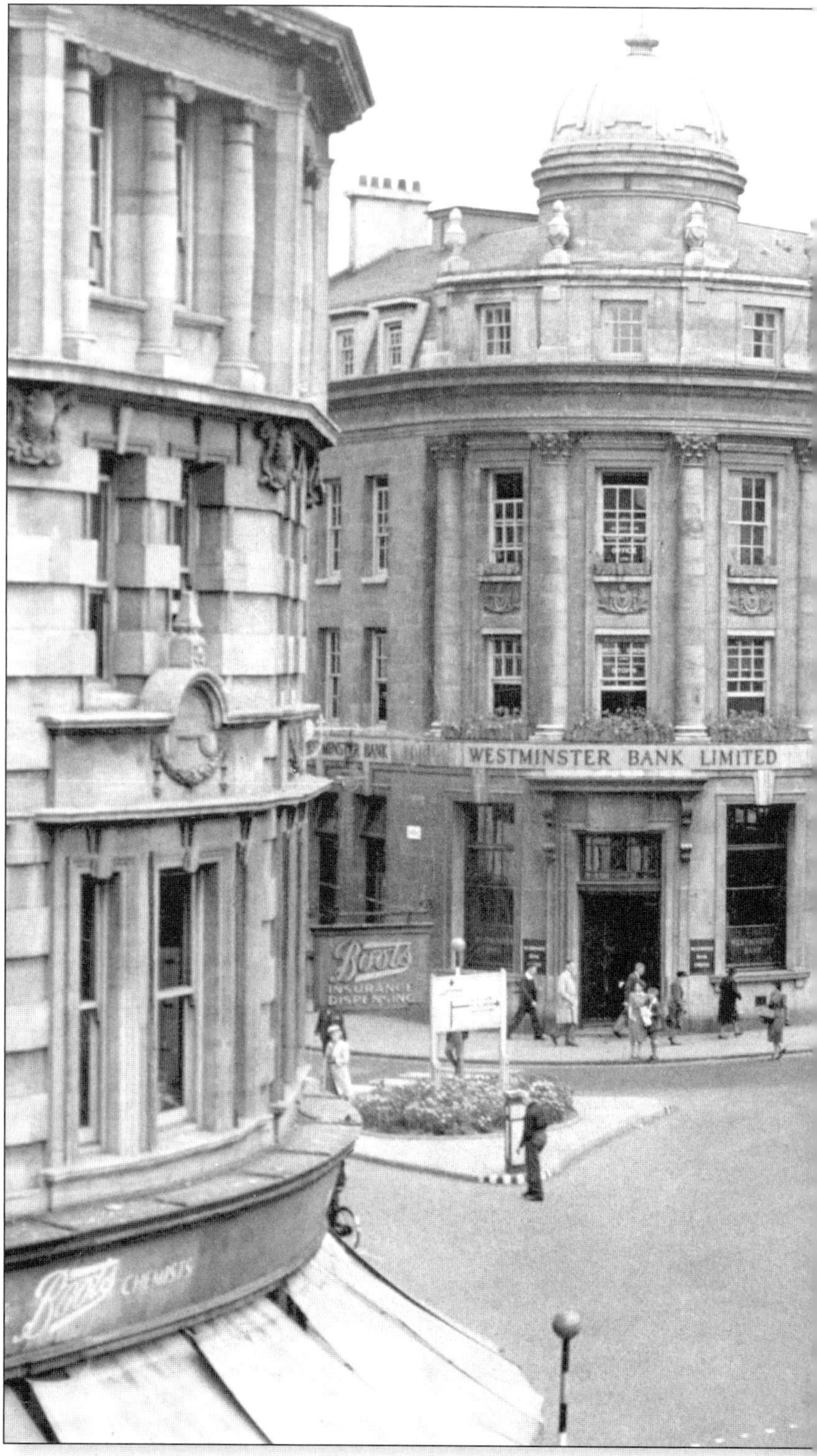

THE TOWN AFTER THE SECOND WORLD WAR

MERCERS ROW c1955 N40018

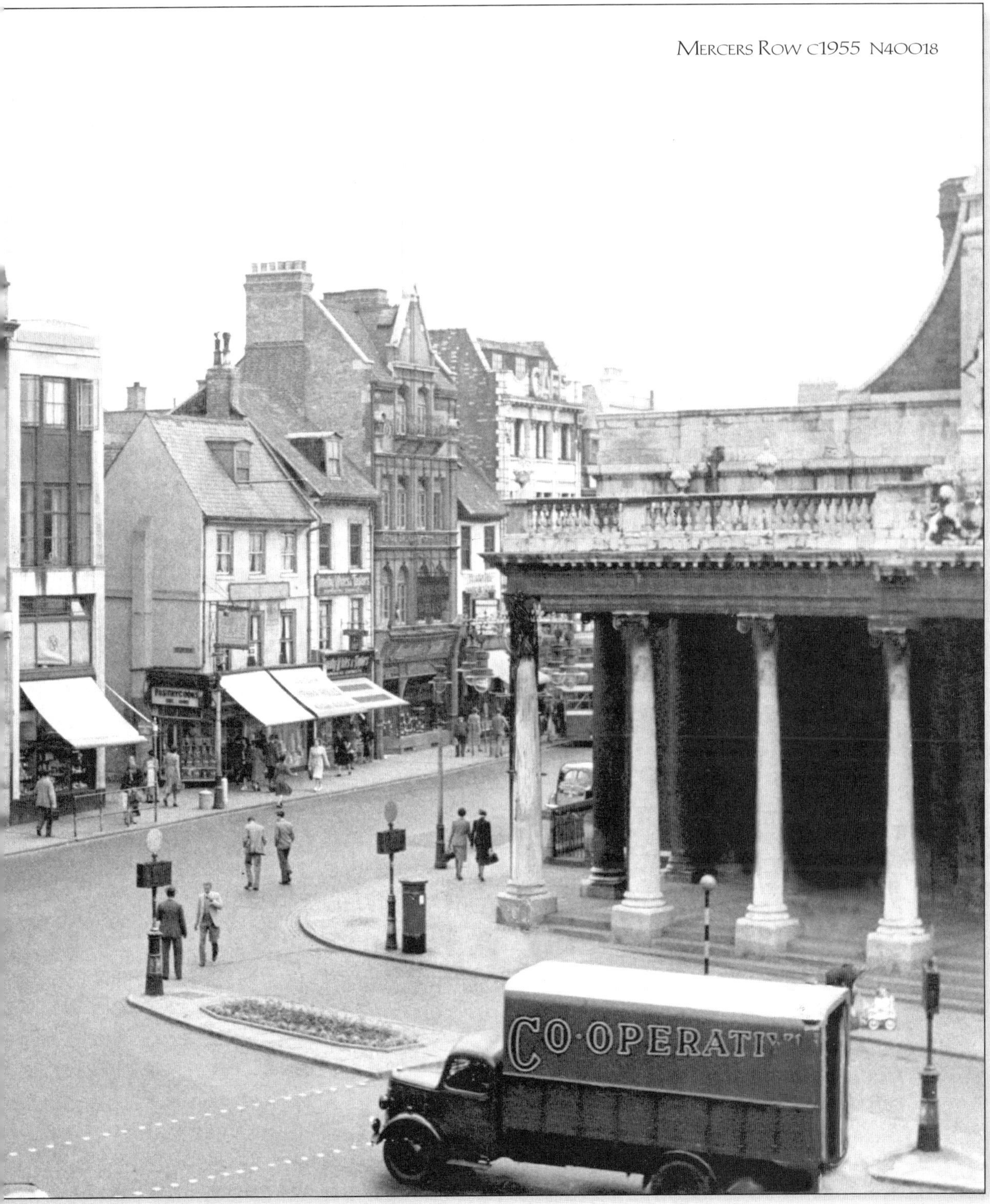

THE TOWN AFTER THE SECOND WORLD WAR

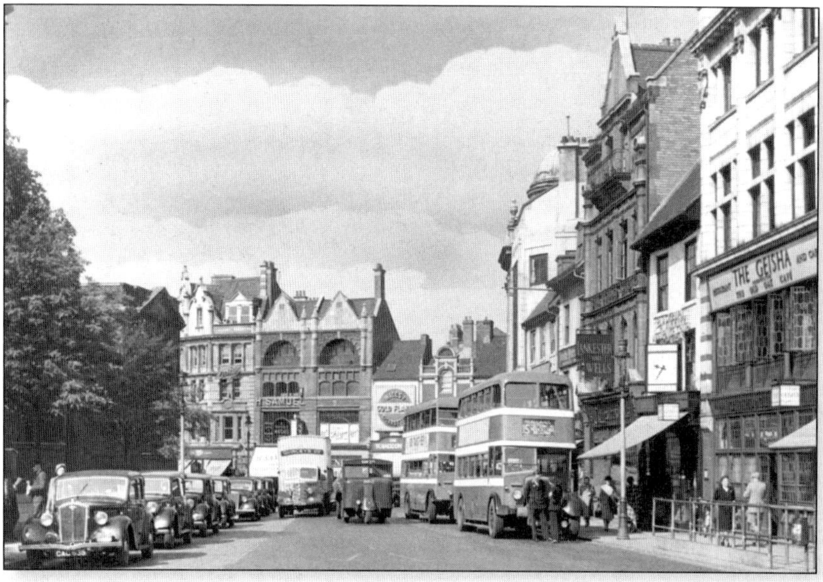

Above: MERCERS ROW c1950 N40001

Right: GOLD STREET c1955 N40057

Note the stylish lettering of T C Palmer on the left-hand corner (we also see it on the right of N40003 below). This view was taken looking west down Gold Street from in front of All Saints' Church. Boots the Chemists have now left County Chambers on the opposite corner.

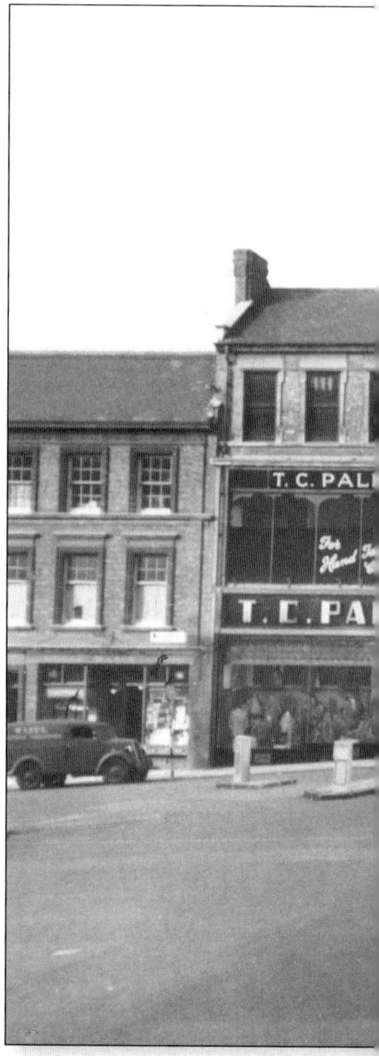

Right: BRIDGE STREET c1955 N40003

Architecturally there has been relatively little change in this and the next two views, apart from down Bridge Street, where the factory we can see in the distance has now gone. On the far left is Lloyds Bank, dated 1923, which faces north on George Row towards All Saints' church.

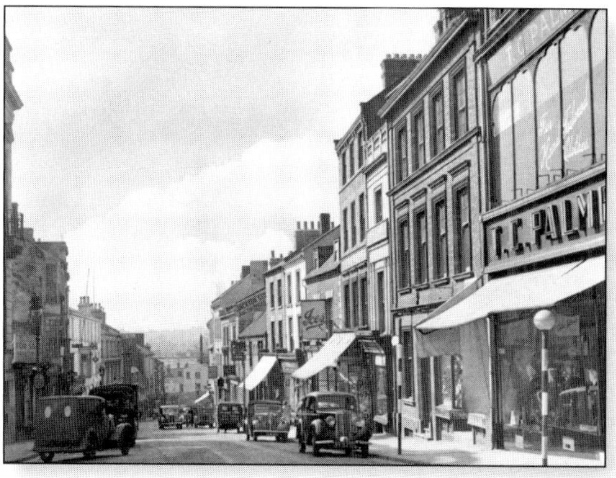

THE TOWN AFTER THE SECOND WORLD WAR

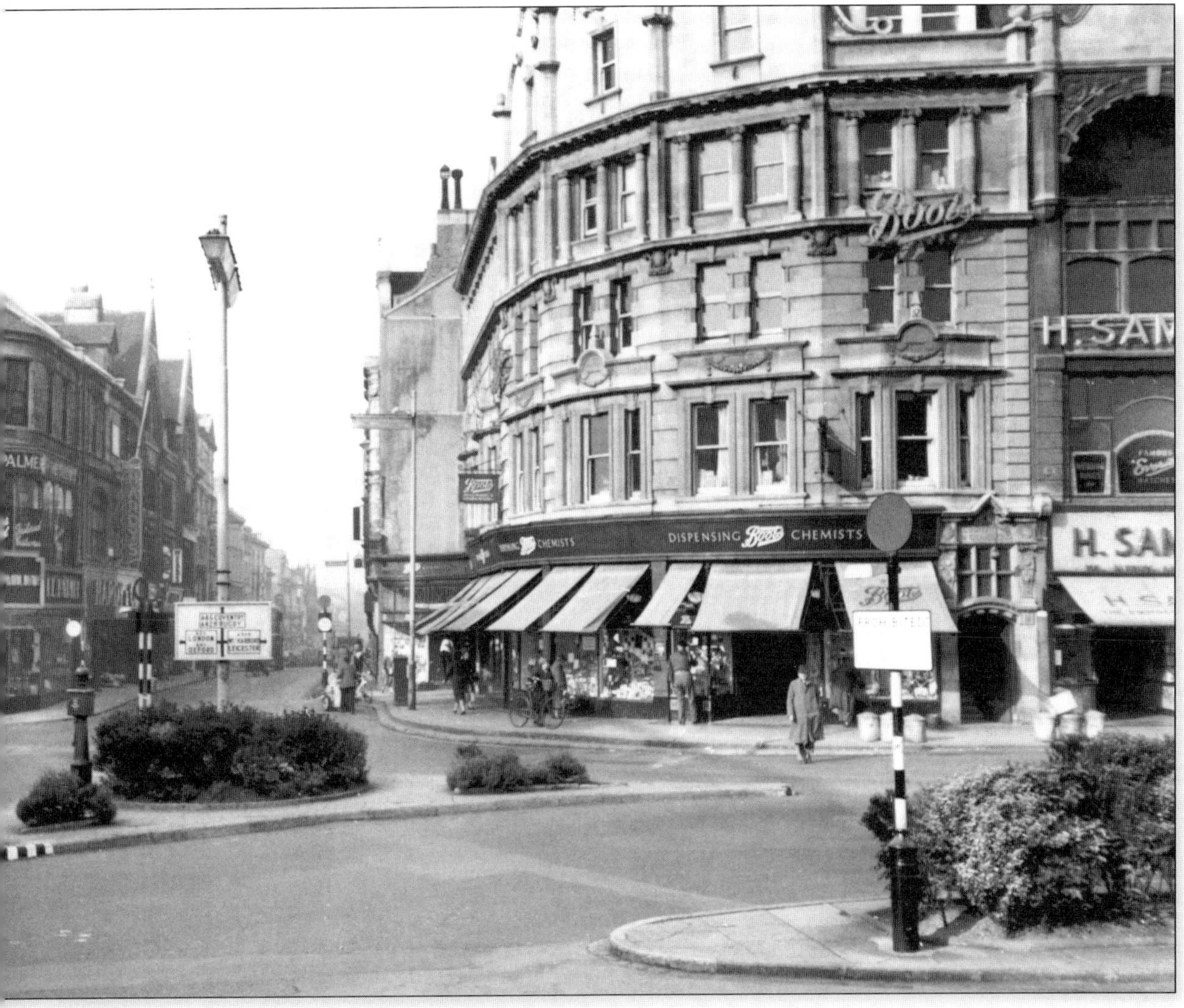

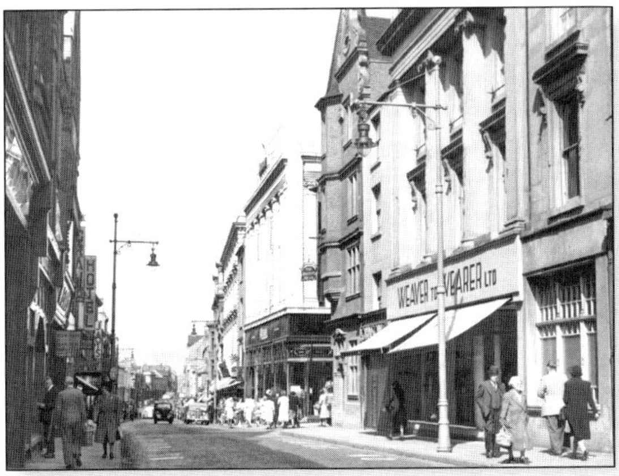

GOLD STREET c1950 N40004

The chain clothes shop Weaver to Wearer is now a Bar Med, and the 1931 Burtons further along has moved on. Note the elegant lamp-posts which replaced the tramway electric cable posts after trams ceased running in the 1930s.

THE TOWN AFTER THE SECOND WORLD WAR

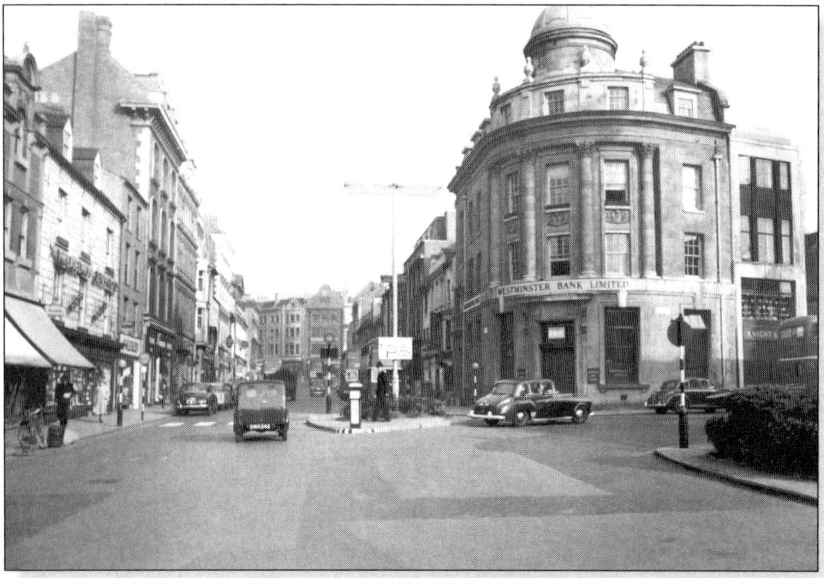

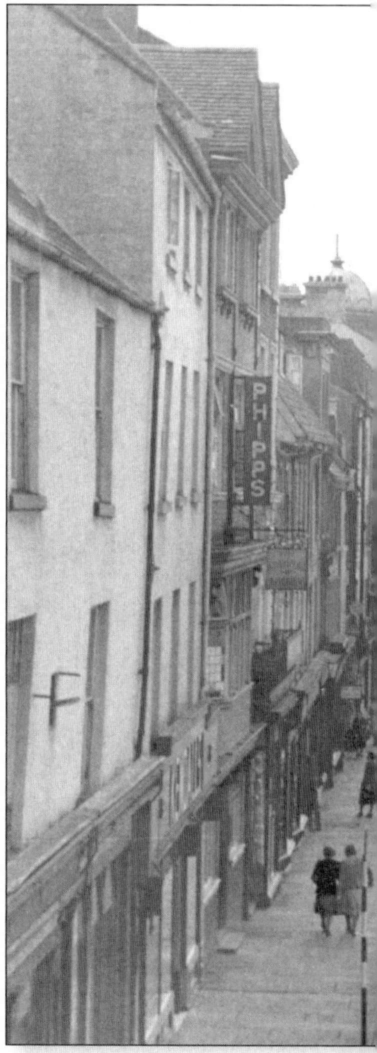

Above: THE DRAPERY C1955 N40056

The Drapery runs parallel to the west side of the Market Place, and was once known as the Glovery. This view was taken from the south beside All Saints' Church. There has been a fair amount of rebuilding since the 1950s, as could be expected in such a busy commercial street, but Philadelphus Jeyes survives. This splendid name is that of a chemist, who opened his shop here in 1810; he was the formulator of Jeyes Fluid, the well-known antiseptic. The shop is still a chemist's.

Above Right: THE DRAPERY C1950 N40005

This view was taken from the north. The superb columned and pedimented former Northamptonshire Union Bank, now a Nat West, dates from 1841.

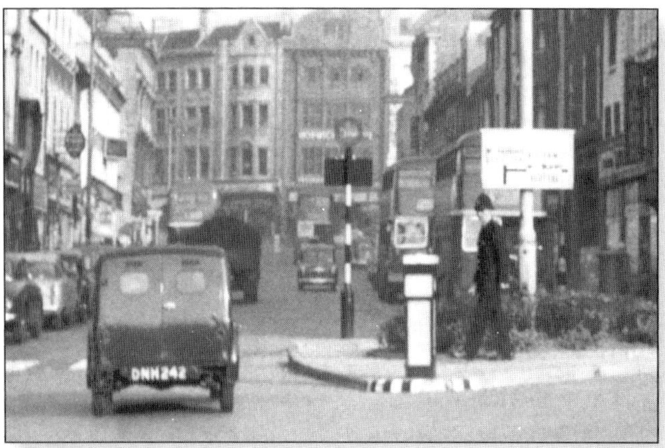

Left: DETAIL FROM N40056

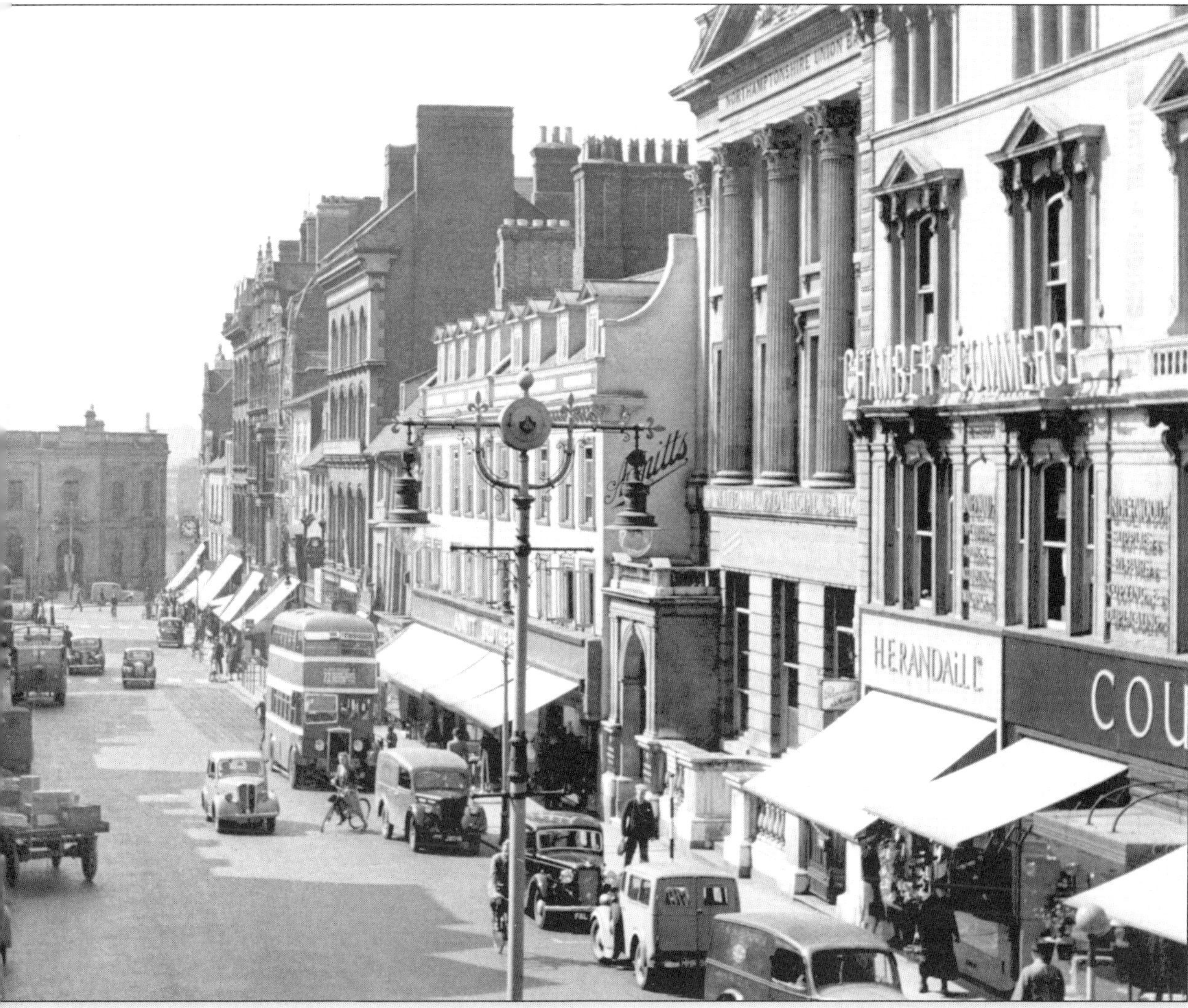

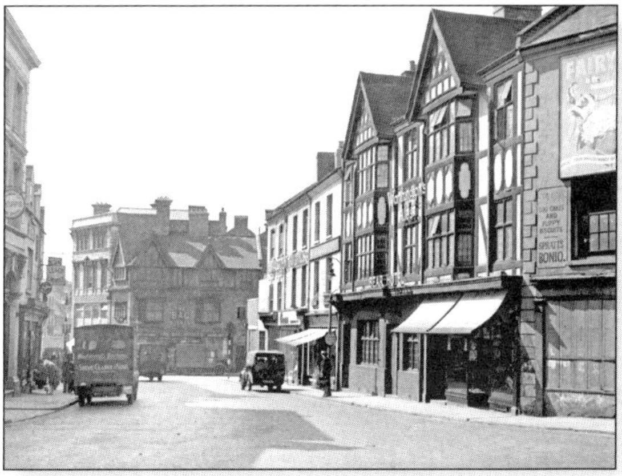

SHEEP STREET C1955 N40007

We are in Sheep Street, looking south towards The Drapery. The architectural quality somewhat falls off at this point with the mock-Tudor Bear Hotel, now just the Bear. In the distance is the Bag Stores of 1901, now Cromwell's Café.

ABINGTON

> *"The Council ... has also recently secured Abington Park, an area of 60 acres or thereabouts, at a cost of £10,000, 20 acres of which ... were the gift of Lord and Lady Wantage. The park is situated in the parish of Abington, at the eastern extremity of the town."*
>
> BRABNER'S GAZETTEER OF ENGLAND AND WALES 1895

The Corporation bought the parkland east of Park Avenue, while the 20 acres of the upper park west of Park Avenue, which contained the former manor house, by then rented as a private mental asylum, was given in 1892 to the Corporation by Lord and Lady Wantage. When the town's boundaries were extended in 1901, they took in the whole of Abington Park.

The park acquired the trappings of a municipal park: a bandstand, duck ponds, flower beds, railings and walks. However, this invaluable asset with its weekend ice cream vans, which is very popular on a sunny afternoon, has at its heart a superb manor house and church. The manor house is now the Abington Museum, which means that as well as looking at the fine local history collections, we can visit and admire its interior. It is administered by the successor to the Corporation, Northampton Borough Council. The views in this chapter show the church, which of course is not in the council's ownership, and the manor house in the 1920s and the 1950s.

Abington's medieval village has long gone; it and its arable land and meadows were largely replaced by the former deer park around the manor house, while the parish church looks for all the world like a private chapel to the house, now that its village

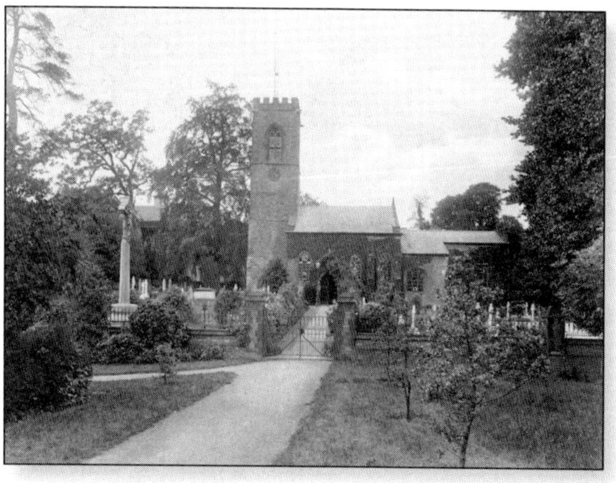

ABINGTON, THE PARISH CHURCH OF ST PETER AND ST PAUL 1922 *72207*

This is a curious church with a tall tower, partly of 1200, with the belfry and battlements 15th-century, and a short boxy nave. This nave is a hybrid of 1821, when the arcades were removed and the lower part of the aisle walls used as the outer walls of the nave. The church is open on some summer Sunday afternoons, and is worth visiting for its superbly-carved pulpit of about 1700.

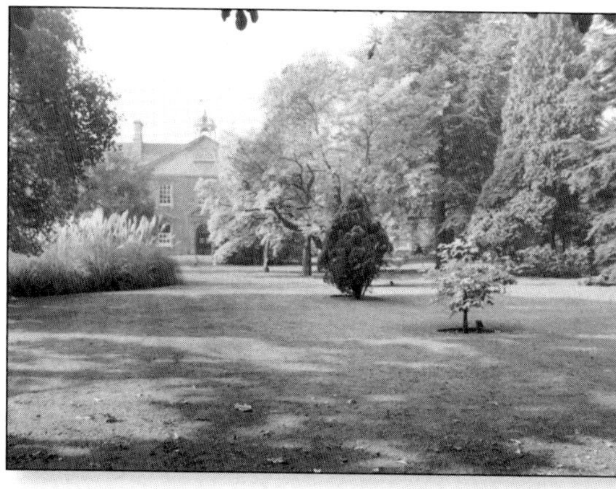

ABINGTON, THE MANOR HOUSE, THE EAST FRONT c1960 N40063

The east front dates from 1738 to 1743; it has a central pediment and a small domed cupola behind. Note the municipal plantings in this view, particularly the pampas grass.

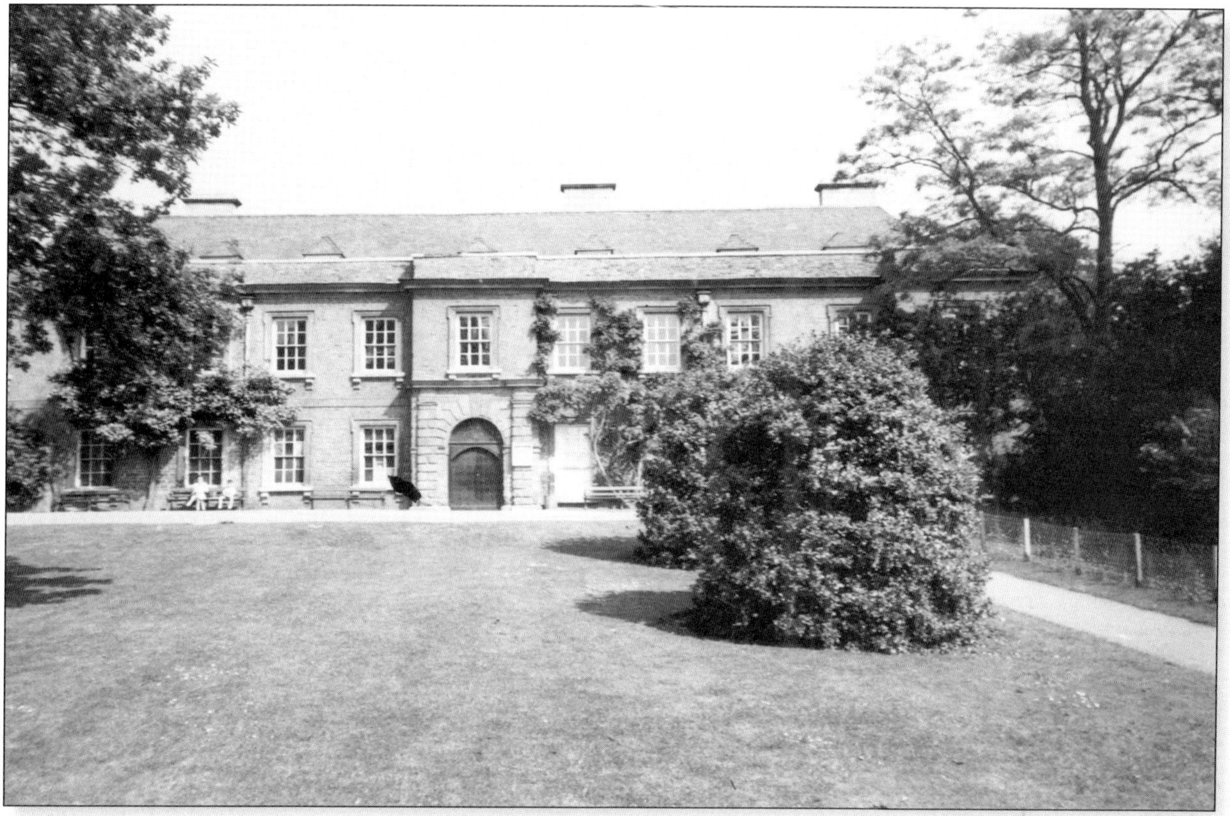

Above: ABINGTON, ABINGTON PARK MUSEUM c1955 N40055

These two views show the south front, with its sash windows of about 1740 inserted into a facade of the 1660s with its rusticated (channelled) pilastered and arched central entrance. The top view shows well the relationship of the manor house to the church.

Right: ABINGTON, THE MANOR HOUSE AND THE CHURCH 1922 72205

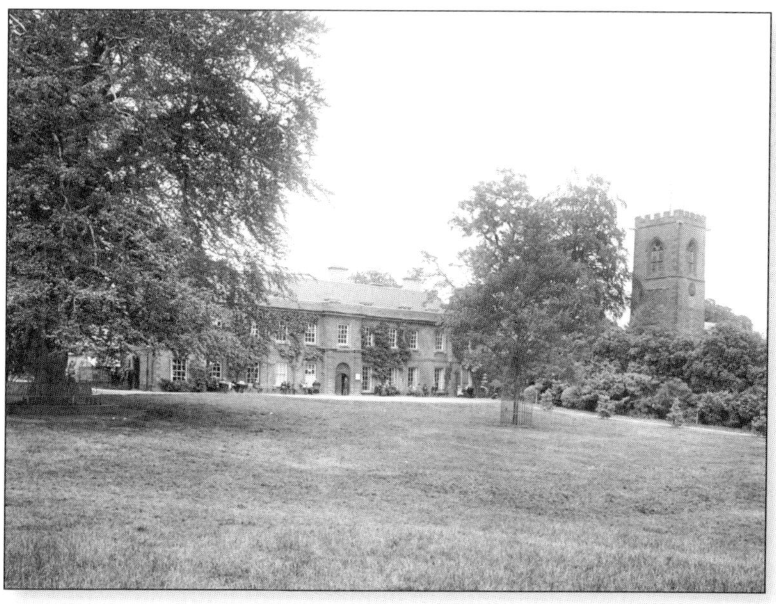

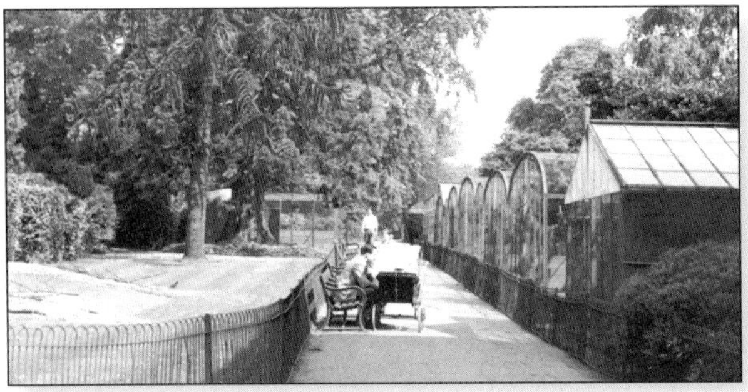

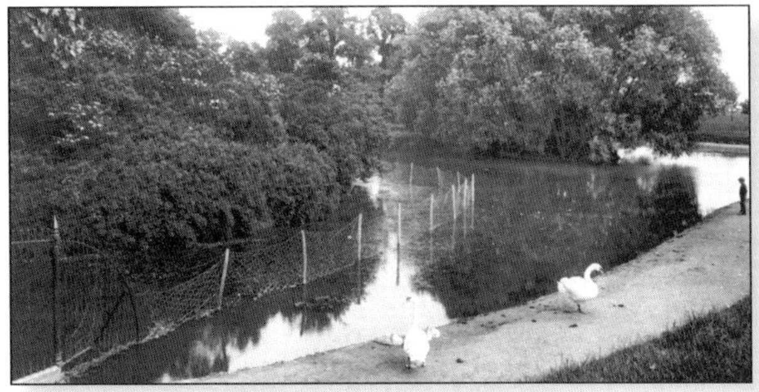

Above Left: ABINGTON PARK
Above Right: THE LAKE 1922 72210

parishioners have vanished (72205, page 79). The earliest parts of the manor house, a fine courtyard house, are to its north-west, largely hidden from the outside view. We enter the museum through a vaulted lobby in the 1660s south range which leads into the reception area and ticket counter. This is the medieval hall of about 1500, built for John Bernard who moved here in 1496, and its great timber hammer-beam roof is its most notable feature. There were once Tudor stables on the north side of the courtyard, but these went after 1892.

The last Bernard built the south range parallel to the Tudor house in the 1660s before selling the estate to the Thursbys in 1669. In 1736 John Harvey, a distant kinsman from Stockton in Warwickshire, inherited; adding Thursby to his name, he set about remodelling the house. He built the east range from 1738 to 1743 (N40063, page 78) — the dates are inscribed on the rainwater hoppers. He apparently used the fashionable architect Francis Smith of Warwick, probably because he knew his work from his years living in Warwickshire. At the same time John Harvey Thursby, as he then was, replaced the south range's casement windows by the then up-to-date and more fashionable sliding sash windows.

The estate was sold by the Thursbys in 1841 to Lewis Loyd of Overstone Park, north-east of Northampton. He let it to a Dr Thomas Octavius Pritchard, who opened the manor house as a private mental asylum. The present-day visitor to the museum will see some fine interiors, particularly the Oak Room with its Tudor linenfold panelling and the grand 1660s staircase.

After Abington Manor House and its grounds were given to the Corporation of Northampton in 1892, it acquired the appurtenances of a municipal recreation ground. These included a fine octagonal bandstand near the Wellingborough Road end of the grounds and an aviary (above). Both survive today, although the aviaries, still popular, were entirely rebuilt a few years ago and now house, among other birds, parakeets, cockatiels, budgerigars, ducks, chickens and pheasants.

In the eastern park, besides the large ponds with their islands for the ducks, geese and swans to roost and breed (above), there is one remarkable survivor of the 17th-century park: isolated on the slopes above the ponds stands a combined dove-house and well house (N40021, page 80), dated 1678 but built in a decidedly medieval style.

The areas north of Abington Park, across the Wellingborough Road, north-east of the artisan housing between Abington Park and the town centre, were developed from the late 19th century as superior housing estates with villas and semi-detached houses. Building continued well into the 1920s. From 1886 the Northamptonshire County Cricket Club ground lay in their midst. The view at the bottom of the page opposite is of a church built to serve one section of this community. In the 20th century, development swept past eastwards to swallow up Weston Favell; and to the south, suburbs such as Abington Vale cut the park off from the countryside for ever.

ABINGTON

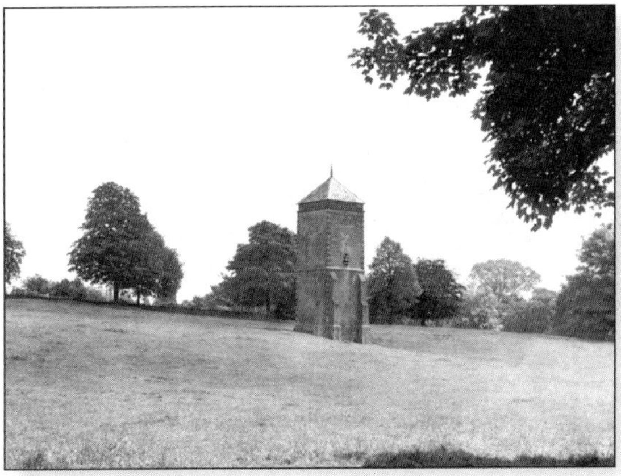

ABINGTON PARK, THE PIGEON TOWER c1955 N40021

Above the ponds in the parkland is the pigeon tower, which was built for William Thursby in 1678. In fact it is a dual-purpose structure, for the lower storey, below the pigeon house, is a well house with a water-wheel pump.

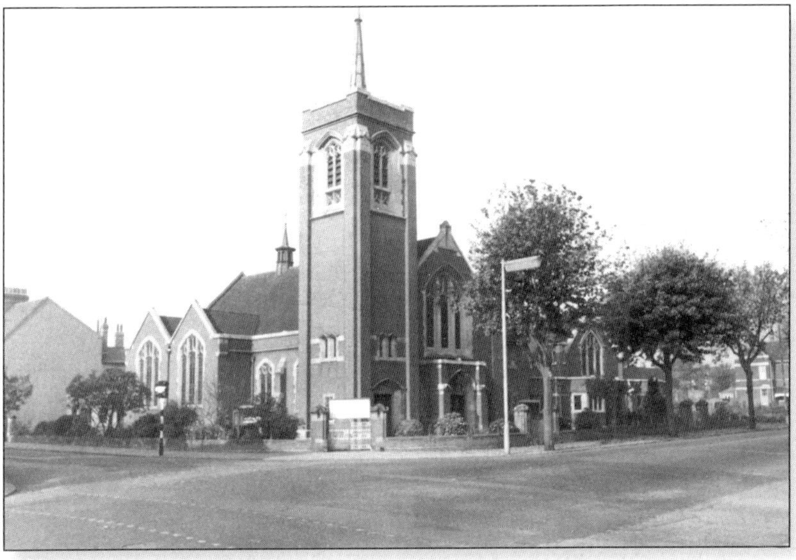

PARK AVENUE METHODIST CHURCH c1960 N40064

Churches were built to serve the suburbs north of Abington Park. This view shows the most striking, the Park Avenue Methodist church, a typical design by George Baines and Son, which dates from 1924. These architects had a prolific practice building non-conformist churches in a late Gothic style, usually in hard red brick with stone dressings, as here. A Baines church usually had a strikingly handsome tower, as this one does.

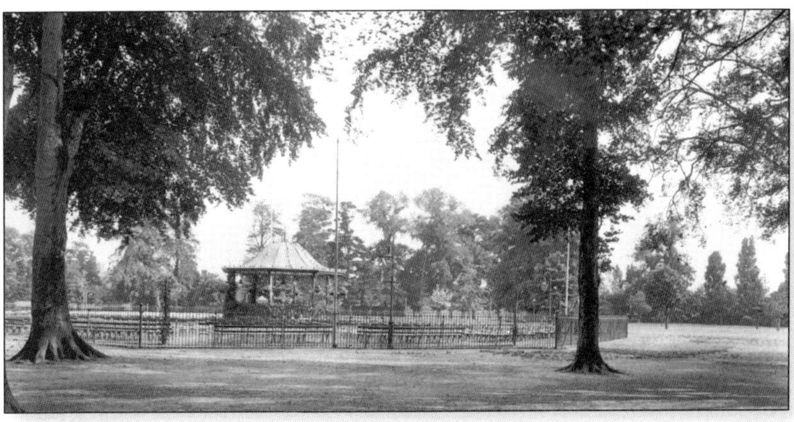

Left: THE BANDSTAND 1922 72208

East of Park Avenue is the forty acres bought by the council for £10,000 in the early 1890s. This descends quite steeply from the road to a couple of large ponds; one is more of a lake, and is studded with well-treed islets for the water fowl to roost and nest.

A BRIEF EXCURSION FROM NORTHAMPTON

"Duston, a parish of Northamptonshire, on the River Nen, adjacent to the Grand Union Canal ... 2 miles W from Northampton. The church is a building of stone in the Early English and Late Decorated styles with traces of Norman, and there is a chapel, which is used by Baptists and Congregationalists."

BRABNER'S GAZETTEER OF ENGLAND AND WALES 1895

Northampton's expansion has taken in a number of villages in its neighbourhood, and this last chapter briefly visits one of them. After a long but ultimately fruitless resistance, Duston was taken into the county borough when the boundary was extended in 1965. Ironically, Duston has had a much longer history than its mighty neighbour, Northampton. It was a settlement area in Neolithic times, judging by the thousands of flint arrowheads and flint tools found hereabouts; it was also a quite important and extensive Roman industrial settlement on a road running south-east from Bannaventa (near Norton) on Watling Street. It grew up to exploit the local ironstone, and it had a flourishing metalworking industry in the 1st and 2nd centuries AD.

Immediately to the west of Duston, and putting a brake on westward expansion, in 1876 Northamptonshire built the vast red brick county lunatic asylum. It was known then as Berrywood Asylum and nowadays, perhaps more tactfully, is called St Crispin's Hospital. This replaced the town's own General Lunatic Asylum on the Billing Road, which opened in 1838 for pauper lunatics. The wealthy lunatic was catered for in private asylums, such as the one in Abington Manor House, which opened in 1845.

Duston village itself, with its medieval parish church, retains quite a lot of stone houses and thatched cottages from its pre-Northampton days; the views in this book record part of it in the 1950s while it was still an independent parish. However, it did have its own industry to its east, with Dallington's housing, incorporated in Northampton's borders in 1901 and 1935, lying immediately beyond. Thus Duston was physically linked to the town long before its formal annexation in 1965.

The final view (72220, page 85) in this book is of one of Northamptonshire's oldest buildings: the west tower doorway of the 10th-century Anglo-Saxon church tower at Earls Barton. The place also had a Norman earthwork castle, a motte and bailey type; in later years it was a boot and shoe making town, one of several that thrived around Northampton.

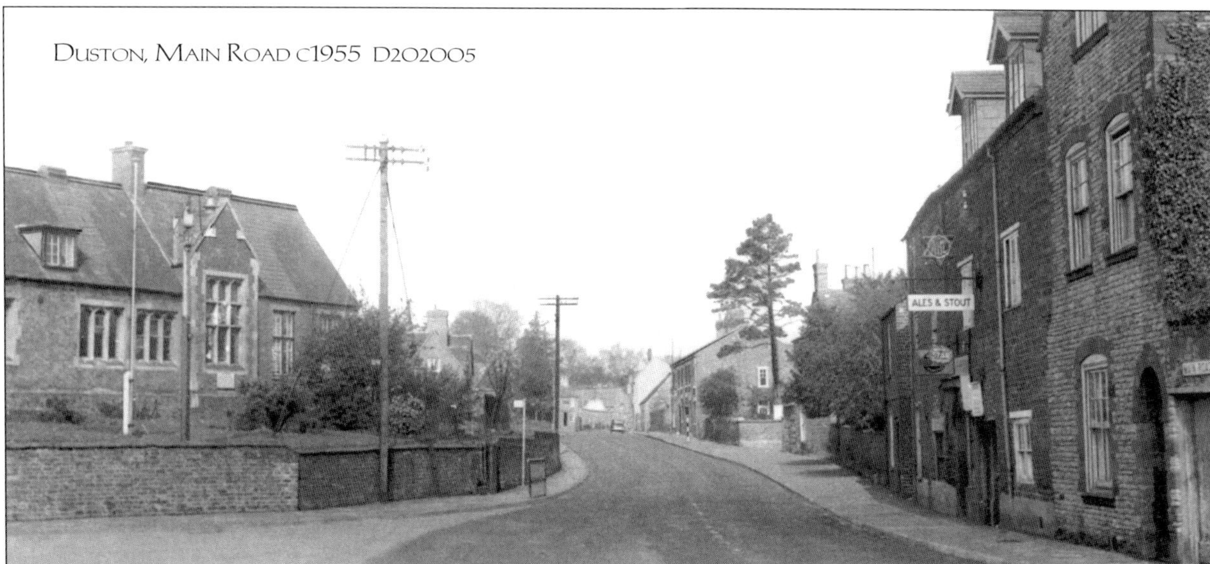

DUSTON, MAIN ROAD c1955 D202005

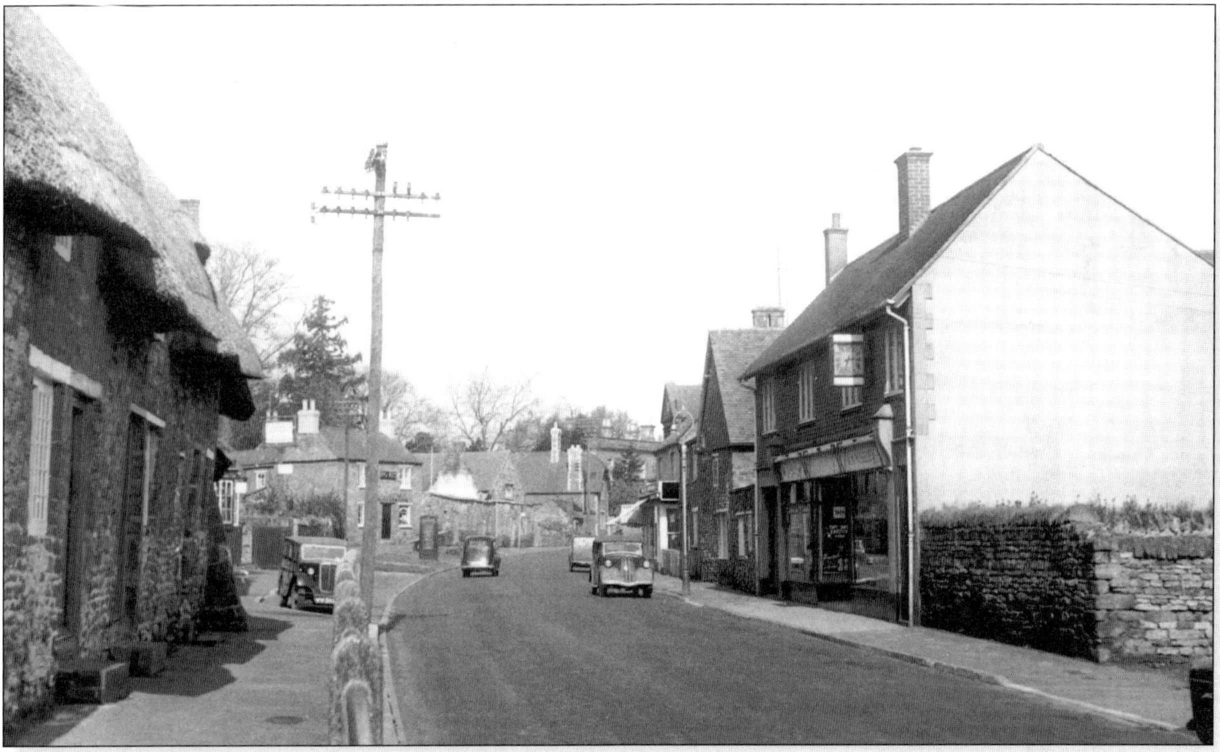

Above: DUSTON, MAIN ROAD c1955 D202009
Below: DETAIL OF D202009

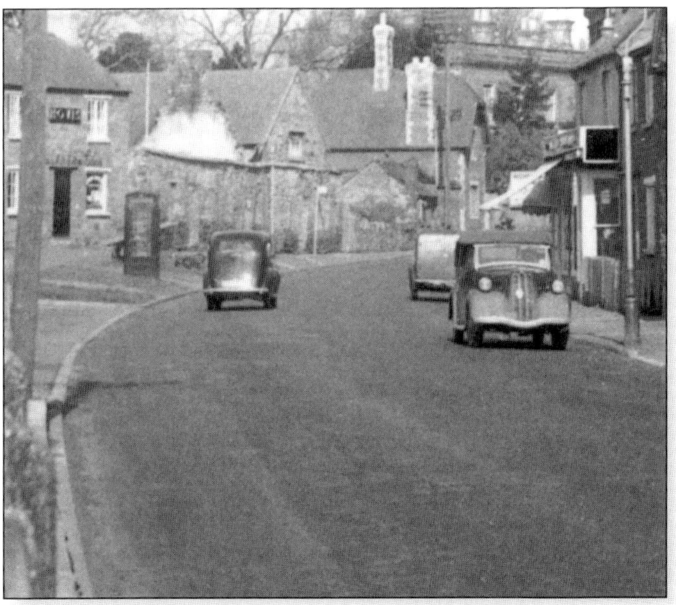

EARLS BARTON

"Most of the inhabitants are engaged in the manufacture of boots and shoes. The church is an ancient building of stone. The tower is a well-known specimen of Saxon building, and the church contains some interesting Norman work and a good 15th-century screen."

BRABNER'S GAZETTEER OF ENGLAND AND WALES 1895

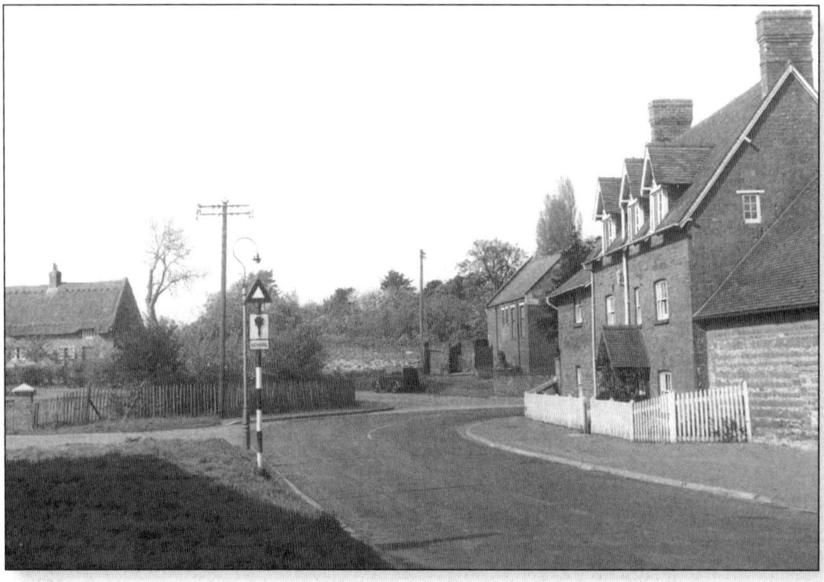

Left: DUSTON, THE VILLAGE c1955 D202013

Below Left: DUSTON, THE SQUIRRELS INN c1955 D202012

These views head west along Main Road from beside the church, view D202013 above, passing the junction with Mill Way and going on past the village school (page 82) erected in 1856, to the thatched pub, the Squirrel Inn. There is quite an architectural mix, with 17th- and 18th-century stone cottages, many thatched, a few larger farmhouses and houses, some Victorian cottages (one pair dated 1875), and more modern ones. The 1950s shop with the clock in view D202009, page 83, has since been demolished and replaced by a larger Co-op store.

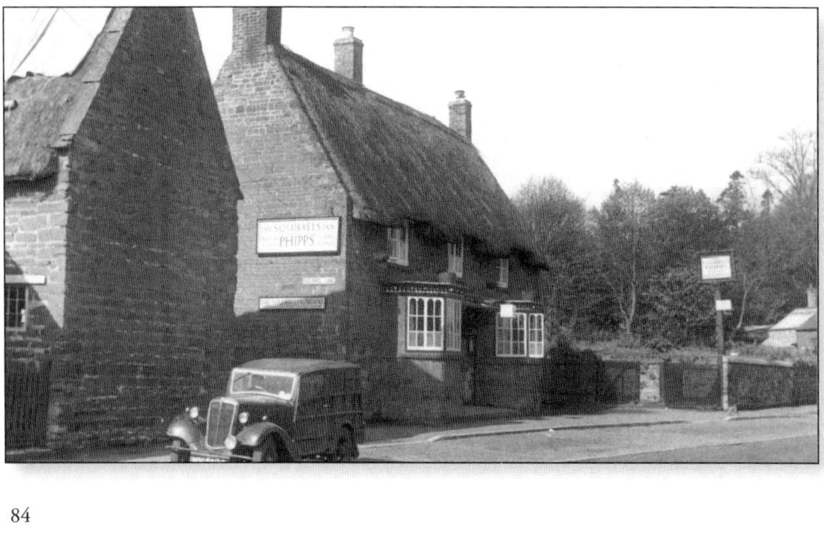

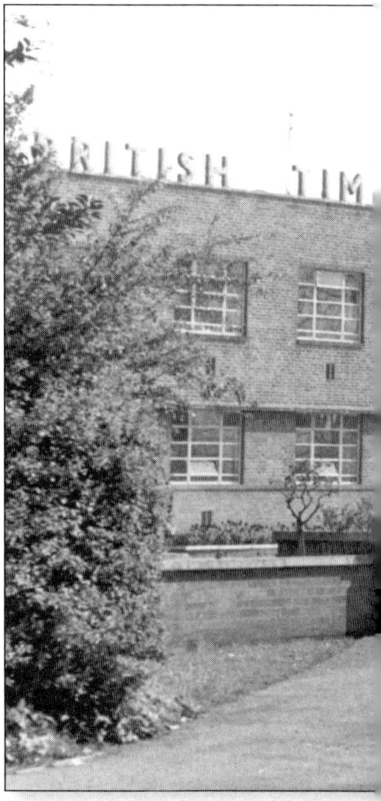

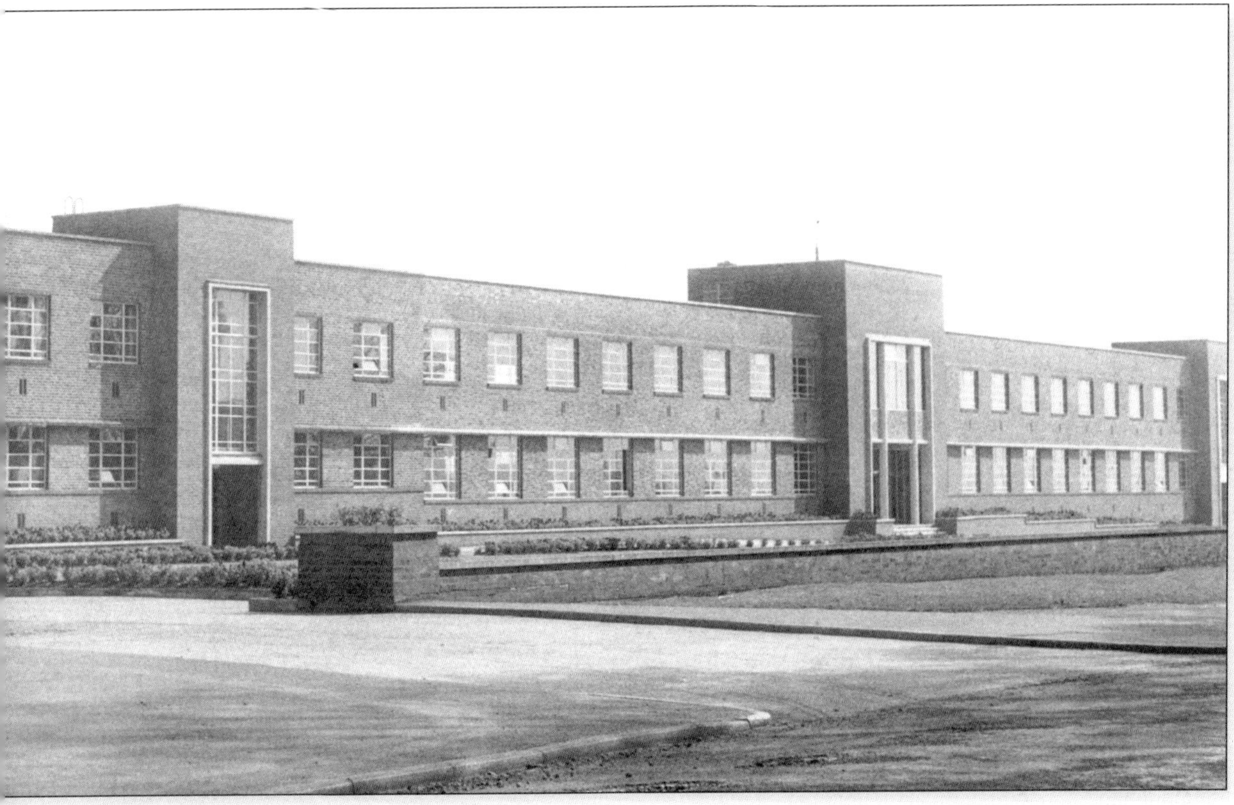

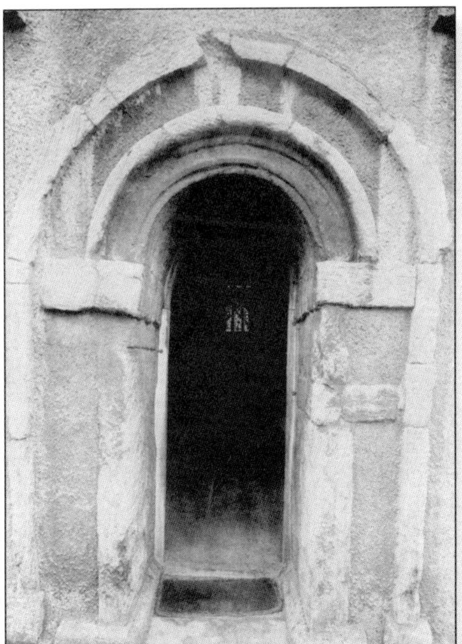

Above: DUSTON, BRITISH TIMKEN c1955 D202019

Just east of the village, where Main Road curves towards Bants Lane, stands this large factory, which employed over 3,000 people in the 1960s. The two-storey office ranges screen the vast factory behind, in which bearings and specialist steel castings and fabrications are made (Northampton was not just boot and shoe factories). British Timken is, in the modern way of things, now just known as Timken. Although the building now has new windows without glazing bars, these elegant offices with their slightly higher projecting pavilions remain as a tribute to the architectural quality and care that could be given to such buildings in the 1930s.

Left: EARLS BARTON, THE CHURCH DOORWAY 1922 72220

This 10th-century doorway with its stone strip decoration gives some idea of the exuberance of the massive Anglo-Saxon tower that adorns this church, which once stood within the outer bailey of a late 11th-century Norman castle that it has long outlived. The tower, with its walls decorated by patterns formed in stone strips, survived the Norman rebuilding of its nave and chancel (although these themselves were much altered later in the Middle Ages). A remarkable survival, the church is one of England's most important Anglo-Saxon monuments.

Names of Subscribers

The following people have kindly supported this book by purchasing limited edition copies prior to publication.

Mr and Mrs D Adams

Michael Bennett, Northampton

To Eddie and Mary Carter, love from Louise

Peter Chambers, Northampton

Leah Williams, love Nan and Pap Chapman

In Memory of Gran, love Kelly and Claire

The Clowes Family, Dymock, Gloucs

The Coleman Family, Northampton

In remembrance of Stan and Vera Collins

Pete and Jan Cropper,Northampton

Peter, Rosemary, Susan and Sarah Daisley

Pete and Michael Dyer

Mark, Emma and Eve Falshaw, Northampton

Mr G N and Mrs J Farrar, Northampton

Mr Roy Finch

To Mum and Dad, love Glenda

Mr F A Goodger, love grandaughter Michelle

For the Halford Family - Brian and Sally

Stuart J Hall, Northampton

Eamonn Hartnett, Northampton

Hazel Hiam, Northampton

The Humphrey Family, Kingsley, Northampton

Peter and Margaret Littler

Mr and Mrs L Maris, Married 2nd April 1956

Mr B J Markie, Mrs A M Markie, Northampton

Mr and Mrs B E Maskell, Northampton

Arthur and Ann Michell, Northampton

William Morrison

Adam Newman

Nicholas Newman

Teresa Louise O'Dell and Family

The Plummer Family, Delapre, Northampton

Nigel Winter Smith, Northampton

The Smith Family, Northampton

To my father Brian Talbot, from Alistair

The Tarrant Family

To Mum, love Emma, Claire and Toby

Mr S W Wixon, Northampton

Victor and Wanda Woodward

INDEX

The Francis Frith Collection Titles

www.francisfrith.co.uk

The Francis Frith Collection publishes over 100 new titles each year. A selection of those currently available is listed below. For latest catalogue please contact The Francis Frith Collection. ***Town Books*** 96 pages, approximately 75 photos. ***County and Themed Books*** 128 pages, approximately 135 photos (unless specified).

Accrington Old and New
Alderley Edge and Wilmslow
Amersham, Chesham and Rickmansworth
Andover
Around Abergavenny
Around Alton
Aylesbury
Barnstaple
Bedford
Bedfordshire
Berkshire Living Memories
Berkshire Pocket Album
Blackpool Pocket Album
Bognor Regis
Bournemouth
Bradford
Bridgend
Bridport
Brighton and Hove
Bristol
Buckinghamshire
Calne Living Memories
Camberley Pocket Album
Canterbury Cathedral
Cardiff Old and New
Chatham and the Medway Towns
Chelmsford
Chepstow Then and Now
Cheshire
Cheshire Living Memories
Chester
Chesterfield
Chigwell
Christchurch
Churches of East Cornwall
Clevedon
Clitheroe
Corby Living Memories
Cornish Coast
Cornwall Living Memories
Cotswold Living Memories
Cotswold Pocket Album
Coulsdon, Chipstead and Woodmanstern
County Durham
Cromer, Sheringham and Holt
Dartmoor Pocket Album
Derby
Derbyshire
Derbyshire Living Memories
Devon
Devon Churches
Dorchester
Dorset Coast Pocket Album
Dorset Living Memories
Dorset Villages
Down the Dart
Down the Severn
Down the Thames
Dunmow, Thaxted and Finchingfield
Durham
East Anglia Pocket Album
East Devon
East Grinstead
Edinburgh
Ely and The Fens
Essex Pocket Album
Essex Second Selection
Essex: The London Boroughs
Exeter
Exmoor
Falmouth
Farnborough, Fleet and Aldershot
Folkestone
Frome
Furness and Cartmel Peninsulas
Glamorgan
Glasgow
Glastonbury
Gloucester
Gloucestershire
Greater Manchester
Guildford
Hailsham
Hampshire
Harrogate
Hastings and Bexhill
Haywards Heath Living Memories
Heads of the Valleys
Heart of Lancashire Pocket Album
Helston
Herefordshire
Horsham
Humberside Pocket Album
Huntingdon, St Neots and St Ives
Hythe, Romney Marsh and Ashford
Ilfracombe
Ipswich Pocket Album
Isle of Wight
Isle of Wight Living Memories
King's Lynn
Kingston upon Thames
Lake District Pocket Album
Lancashire Living Memories
Lancashire Villages

Available from your local bookshop or from the publisher

The Francis Frith Collection Titles (continued)

Lancaster, Morecambe and Heysham Pocket Album
Leeds Pocket Album
Leicester
Leicestershire
Lincolnshire Living Memoires
Lincolnshire Pocket Album
Liverpool and Merseyside
London Pocket Album
Ludlow
Maidenhead
Maidstone
Malmesbury
Manchester Pocket Album
Marlborough
Matlock
Merseyside Living Memories
Nantwich and Crewe
New Forest
Newbury Living Memories
Newquay to St Ives
North Devon Living Memories
North London
North Wales
North Yorkshire
Northamptonshire
Northumberland
Northwich
Nottingham
Nottinghamshire Pocket Album
Oakham
Odiham Then and Now
Oxford Pocket Album
Oxfordshire
Padstow
Pembrokeshire
Penzance
Petersfield Then and Now
Plymouth
Poole and Sandbanks
Preston Pocket Album
Ramsgate Old and New
Reading Pocket Album
Redditch Living Memories
Redhill to Reigate
Richmond
Ringwood
Rochdale
Romford Pocket Album
Salisbury Pocket Album
Scotland
Scottish Castles
Sevenoaks and Tonbridge
Sheffield and South Yorkshire Pocket Album
Shropshire
Somerset
South Devon Coast
South Devon Living Memories
South East London
Southampton Pocket Album
Southend Pocket Album
Southport
Southwold to Aldeburgh
Stourbridge Living Memories
Stratford upon Avon
Stroud
Suffolk
Suffolk Pocket Album
Surrey Living Memories
Sussex
Sutton
Swanage and Purbeck
Swansea Pocket Album
Swindon Living Memories
Taunton
Teignmouth
Tenby and Saundersfoot
Tiverton
Torbay
Truro
Uppingham
Villages of Kent
Villages of Surrey
Villages of Sussex Pocket Album
Wakefield and the Five Towns Living Memories
Warrington
Warwick
Warwickshire Pocket Album
Wellingborough Living Memories
Wells
Welsh Castles
West Midlands Pocket Album
West Wiltshire Towns
West Yorkshire
Weston-super-Mare
Weymouth
Widnes and Runcorn
Wiltshire Churches
Wiltshire Living Memories
Wiltshire Pocket Album
Wimborne
Winchester Pocket Album
Windermere
Windsor
Wirral
Wokingham and Bracknell
Woodbridge
Worcester
Worcestershire
Worcestershire Living Memories
Wyre Forest
York Pocket Album
Yorkshire
Yorkshire Coastal Memories
Yorkshire Dales
Yorkshire Revisited

Frith Products & Services

Francis Frith would doubtless be pleased to know that the pioneering publishing venture he started in 1860 still continues today. Over a hundred and forty years later, The Francis Frith Collection continues in the same innovative tradition and is now one of the foremost publishers of vintage photographs in the world. Some of the current activities include:

Interior Decoration

Today Frith's photographs can be seen framed and as giant wall murals in thousands of pubs, restaurants, hotels, banks, retail stores and other public buildings throughout the country. In every case they enhance the unique local atmosphere of the places they depict and provide reminders of gentler days in an increasingly busy and frenetic world.

Product Promotions

Frith products are used by many major companies to promote the sales of their own products or to reinforce their own history and heritage. Frith promotions have been used by Hovis bread, Courage beers, Scots Porage Oats, Colman's mustard, Cadbury's foods, Mellow Birds coffee, Dunhill pipe tobacco, Guinness, and Bulmer's Cider.

Genealogy and Family History

As the interest in family history and roots grows world-wide, more and more people are turning to Frith's photographs of Great Britain for images of the towns, villages and streets where their ancestors lived; and, of course, photographs of the churches and chapels where their ancestors were christened, married and buried are an essential part of every genealogy tree and family album.

Frith Products

All Frith photographs are available Framed or just as Mounted Prints and Posters (size 23 x 16 inches). These may be ordered from the address below. From time to time other products - Address Books, Calendars, Table Mats, etc - are available.

The Internet

Already ninety thousand Frith photographs can be viewed and purchased on the internet through the Frith websites and a myriad of partner sites.

For more detailed information on Frith companies and products, look at these sites:

www.francisfrith.co.uk
www.francisfrith.com
(for North American visitors)

See the complete list of Frith Books at:

www.francisfrith.co.uk

This web site is regularly updated with the latest list of publications from The Francis Frith Collection. If you wish to buy books relating to another part of the country that your local bookshop does not stock, you may purchase on-line.

For further information, trade, or author enquiries please contact us at the address below:

The Francis Frith Collection, Frith's Barn, Teffont, Salisbury, Wiltshire, England SP3 5QP.
Tel: +44 (0)1722 716 376 Fax: +44 (0)1722 716 881 Email: sales@francisfrith.co.uk

See Frith books on the internet at www.francisfrith.co.uk

FREE PRINT OF YOUR CHOICE

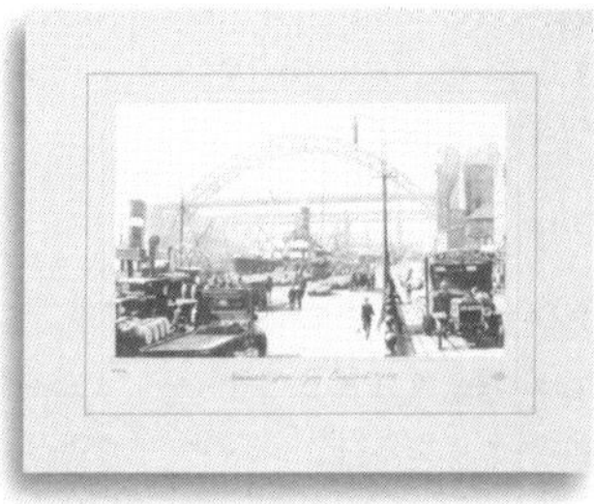

Mounted Print
Overall size 14 x 11 inches (355 x 280mm)

Choose any Frith photograph in this book.
Simply complete the Voucher opposite and return it with your remittance for £2.25 (to cover postage and handling) and we will print the photograph of your choice in SEPIA (size 11 x 8 inches) and supply it in a cream mount with a burgundy rule line (overall size 14 x 11 inches).
Please note: photographs with a reference number starting with a "Z" are not Frith photographs and cannot be supplied under this offer.
Offer valid for delivery to one UK address only.

***PLUS:* Order additional Mounted Prints at HALF PRICE - £7.49 each** (normally £14.99)
If you would like to order more Frith prints from this book, possibly as gifts for friends and family, you can buy them at half price (with no additional postage and handling costs).

***PLUS:* Have your Mounted Prints framed**
For an extra £14.95 per print you can have your mounted print(s) framed in an elegant polished wood and gilt moulding, overall size 16 x 13 inches (no additional postage and handling required).

IMPORTANT!

These special prices are only available if you use this form to order. You must use the ORIGINAL VOUCHER on this page (no copies permitted). We can only despatch to one UK address. This offer cannot be combined with any other offer.

Send completed Voucher form to:
The Francis Frith Collection, Frith's Barn, Teffont, Salisbury, Wiltshire SP3 5QP

CHOOSE A PHOTOGRAPH FROM THIS BOOK

Voucher *for **FREE** and Reduced Price Frith Prints*

Please do not photocopy this voucher. Only the original is valid, so please fill it in, cut it out and return it to us with your order.

Picture ref no	Page no	Qty	Mounted @ £7.49	Framed + £14.95	Total Cost £
		1	Free of charge*	£	£
			£7.49	£	£
			£7.49	£	£
			£7.49	£	£
			£7.49	£	£
			£7.49	£	£
			* Post & handling		£3.50
			Total Order Cost		£

Please allow 28 days for delivery.
Offer available to one UK address only

Title of this book ....
I enclose a cheque/postal order for £ ....
made payable to 'The Francis Frith Collection'

OR please debit my Mastercard / Visa / Maestro / Amex card, details below

Card Number

Issue No (Maestro only) Valid from (Maestro)

Expires Signature

Name Mr/Mrs/Ms ....
Address ....
....
....
.... Postcode ....
Daytime Tel No ....
Email ....

ISBN 1-84589-037-X Valid to 31/12/08

Free Print - see overleaf

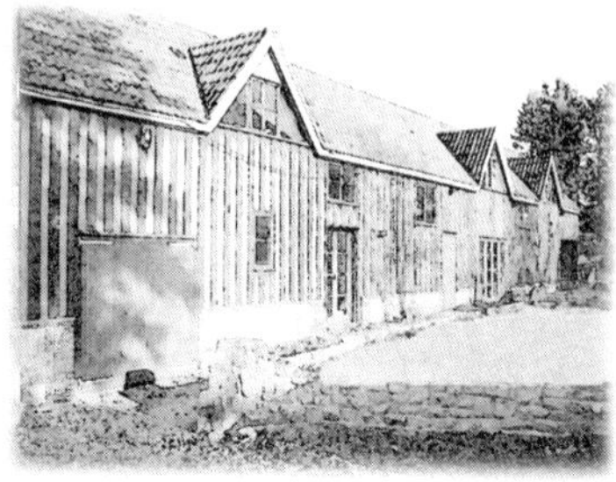

Can you help us with information about any of the Frith photographs in this book?

We are gradually compiling an historical record for each of the photographs in the Frith archive. It is always fascinating to find out the names of the people shown in the pictures, as well as insights into the shops, buildings and other features depicted.

If you recognize anyone in the photographs in this book, or if you have information not already included in the author's caption, do let us know. We would love to hear from you, and will try to publish it in future books or articles.

Our production team

Frith books are produced by a small dedicated team at offices in the converted Grade II listed 18th-century barn at Teffont near Salisbury, illustrated above. Most have worked with the Frith Collection for many years. All have in common one quality: they have a passion for the Frith Collection. The team is constantly expanding, but currently includes:

Paul Baron, Jason Buck, John Buck, Ruth Butler, Heather Crisp, David Davies, Louis du Mont, Isobel Hall, Lucy Hart, Julian Hight, Peter Horne, James Kinnear, Karen Kinnear, Tina Leary, Stuart Login, Sue Molloy, Sarah Roberts, Kate Rotondetto, Dean Scource, Eliza Sackett, Terence Sackett, Sandra Sampson, Adrian Sanders, Sandra Sanger, Julia Skinner, Miles Smith, Lewis Taylor, Shelley Tolcher, Lorraine Tuck, Miranda Tunnicliffe, David Turner and Ricky Williams.